RED, WHITE AND RADICAL

Red, White and Radical explores how and why America has become so conservative since World War II. In the process, it offers lessons that professional leaders, regardless of their political stance, should heed if they want their organisational change plans to succeed.

Over the past 70 years, a motley crew of suburban activists, libertarian businessmen and political opportunists have radically changed America and its national values. The rise of American conservatism is the greatest modern example of cultural change in the Western world. How did they do it – and what can we learn from this? *Red, White and Radical* is a manual for organisational change. It tells nine stories from American cultural, political and business history that illuminate how conservatives have pioneered change. From these stories, it extracts a change management lesson for professional leaders and explains how to apply that lesson in the workplace.

These nine lessons are organised into a clear change framework:

1. understanding and motivating people
2. communicating with emotion and authenticity
3. building teams and networks that can deliver lasting change.

Along the way you'll also learn:

- how Marlboro became the world's biggest cigarette brand
- why conservatives love Ronald Reagan but despise Richard Nixon
- the origins of the social media echo chamber
- how Silicon Valley learned to lobby
- the secrets of Donald Trump's populist X Factor.

Red, White and Radical is not for the faint of heart. If you're a passionate business leader who relishes the challenge of delivering true organisational change for the better, then this book is for you.

WARRICK HARNIESS is an educator and founder of Scandinavia Stories, a learning and development agency that specialises in creativity, communications and change. His clients include multinational companies and professional services firms, universities and start-ups. He learned his craft during a career at Pearson Education, and as a musician inspired by punk rock and the do-it-yourself ethos. *Red, White and Radical* is his first book.

RED, WHITE AND RADICAL

WHAT ORGANISATIONS CAN LEARN ABOUT CHANGE FROM THE RISE OF AMERICAN CONSERVATISM

Warrick Harniess

Routledge
Taylor & Francis Group

LONDON AND NEW YORK

First published 2020
by Routledge
2 Park Square, Milton Park, Abingdon, Oxon OX14 4RN

and by Routledge
52 Vanderbilt Avenue, New York, NY 10017

Routledge is an imprint of the Taylor & Francis Group, an informa business

British Library Cataloguing-in-Publication Data
A catalogue record for this book is available from the British Library

Library of Congress Cataloging-in-Publication Data
A catalog record has been requested for this book

ISBN: 978-0-367-14971-0 (hbk)
ISBN: 978-0-429-05419-8 (ebk)

Typeset in Minion Pro and Helvetica Neue
by Swales & Willis, Exeter, Devon, UK

For my family

CONTENTS

CONTENTS

'Cultural change is hard'
President Donald J. Trump, 5 August 2019

IMAGES

ABOUT THE AUTHOR

Warrick Harniess is an educator and founder of Scandinavia Stories, a learning and development agency that specialises in creativity, communications and change. His clients include multinational companies and professional services firms, universities and start-ups.

He learned his craft during a career at Pearson Education, and as a musician inspired by punk rock and the do-it-yourself ethos.

Red, White and Radical is his first book.

Contact the author: warrick@scandinaviastories.co.uk

scandinaviastories.co.uk

Introduction

Culture change is no joke, but it is laughably hard to get right. Meaning, if your boss gives you the poisoned chalice of heading up a culture-change programme you can only accept the challenge with good humour and a steely resolve. It's either a sign that you're in the running for a big promotion, or an omen that your days at the company have been designed to be limited.

In 2010 I was kind of a rising star at Pearson Education. At least, that was how I saw myself and I was determined to prove myself one (spoiler: I went off the rails and fell out with the kingmakers). Organisational culture change was all the rage, and anyone who was anyone wanted to be involved in efforts to make it happen. Someone in the corridors of power recommended I read Lynda Gratton's book *Hot Spots* so I could learn more about leading change.

Lynda is a highly decorated business thinker and a professor at London Business School. *Hot Spots* was published in 2007 and outlined a method for harnessing areas of creativity and productivity within the organisation ('hot spots') and spreading that energy throughout the rest of the company. *Hot Spots* drew on her research with industry-leading companies such as Goldman Sachs, Nokia and BP. It was interesting, except that a lot had happened between 2007 and 2010 that put a bit of a damper on the advice it offered.

In 2008, the American government rescued Goldman Sachs from the brink of bankruptcy. In the political and cultural fallout from the financial crisis it was found to have defrauded investors and was famously called a 'great vampire squid wrapped around the face of humanity' by journalist Matt Taibi.

In 2007, upon the launch of the iPhone, Nokia's share of the mobile phone market began to fall from a peak of 49%. It fell fast, and when Microsoft bought its mobile business in 2013 it had just 3% of the market. Analysts concluded that Nokia's culture had grown fat, contented and complacent with success. Steve Jobs was lean and mean, and Apple had a point to prove.

And in 2010, an explosion on a BP-contracted drilling rig in the Gulf of Mexico killed 11 people and caused the biggest ever marine oil spill. Shares in BP tumbled and CEO Tony Hayward, brought in three years earlier to oversee a culture change, was pilloried for telling the media, 'I'd like my life back' and going yachting in the midst of the crisis. Hayward resigned in disgrace, and BP was criminally indicted by the US Department of Justice.

Harnessing energy and spreading creativity around an organisation is hard to do. Working out how to do it successfully requires a pretty good understanding of people. But clearly that alone isn't enough to guarantee lasting culture change.

THE GREAT GAME OF BUSINESS

Four years after reading *Hot Spots* I decided that corporate life was no longer for me and quit my job to pursue entrepreneurial independence. To celebrate my uncertain future, my sister bought me a book, *The Great Game of Business*, by Jack Stack and Bo Burlingham. As a blueprint for the way forward for me, it was useless. But another four years after I first read it, I remembered that it was probably the best example of successful organisational change that I'd ever come across.

The story of Springfield Remanufacturing Corporation is a classic business turnaround case study of the underdog triumphing against the odds. Jack Stack was a manager at the International Harvester ReNew Center in Springfield, Missouri. The ReNew Center rebuilt engines for the agricultural machinery that Harvester made, but by the early 1980s Harvester, once one of America's biggest manufacturers, was struggling. As he tells it, Jack hoped to save 119 jobs, including his own. Together with 12 other managers they scraped together $100,000 with the hope of borrowing $9 million to meet the buyout price that Harvester wanted for the ReNew Center.

> We went out to 50 financial institutions in the United States looking for money, and we took our silly little resumes and our innocent little business plans and we were about as naïve as anybody came. We were taught to be good manufacturers. We were never taught to be business people. And so we kept getting turned down because we were economically illiterate. You know what the banks wanna know?

Stack smirks and exaggerates the pernickety nasal tone of a bank loan manager:

> When am I gonna pay back the money? They didn't care about the customer! All they cared about were financial ratios. And I kept saying to myself, 'if this is the definition of job security, if this is what we were supposed to be doing all these 14 years we worked for this company, why didn't anybody tell us?'

Incredibly, Stack and his fellow managers were eventually able to raise the money they needed. With an eye-watering debt-to-equity ratio of 89:1, Springfield Remanufacturing Corporation (SRC) was born. Still smarting from his experience with the banks, Stack resolved to run SRC differently. With so much money to repay and its stock valued at just ten cents per share, Stack created the Employee Stock Ownership Plan (ESOP). If the company was to prosper, his employees would have to have a true stake in the game. They would need to be owners, and in order to be owners they would need to understand how and why managers made decisions.

Jack's change method came to be known as open-book management. Blue-collar workers were taught how to read financial reports and balance sheets, and, through familiarity with how their areas of responsibility contributed to the company's financial results, to accurately forecast and plan. Stack proved a canny entrepreneur, and in the 35 years since, SRC has created and spun off sixty more companies, many to former employees. Its stock is now worth hundreds of dollars per share.

Stack himself called his approach the great game of business, or GGOB for short. GGOB has been recognised as a culture-change method that works and lauded by *The Economist, Harvard Business Review, Wall Street Journal, Entrepreneur Magazine, Forbes* and the *New York Times* amongst others.

CULTURE IS A MORAL SYSTEM

Jack Stack understood that culture is a way of seeing the world that influences behaviour. If managers and employees share the same worldview, then they are more likely to agree about what could be called a natural order of things, and less likely to get into disputes about what is and isn't fair and right.

Sharing the same worldview isn't the same as having the same individual goals or expectations. Organisations are hierarchical, and most of us accept that the more senior you are in a company the more you should get paid, and the more senior you become the more responsibility you'll bear. Often we don't agree with how this works in practice, because we're not satisfactorily told why certain people have been promoted. We say indignantly to ourselves (or anyone who'll listen): 'they're not that smart or hard working – they're just the professional equivalent of a teacher's pet!' We may or may not be justified in thinking this way about own abilities in comparison to the person who got promoted over us, but when we do feel this way it's possible we're reacting to a reality: culture rewards those who fit in, limits those who don't and punishes those who transgress.

Culture is both ideological and pragmatic, which is basically another way of saying that there are rules but for every rule there can always be an exception. Culture is powerful because individuals are selected and indoctrinated so well, without much conscious intent, and the culture then asserts itself through the actions of thousands of people. The rules are essentially unwritten, and the ways to break the rules to your advantage are never clear. This goes for anyone in an organisation, regardless of seniority. Think about how many CEOs are brought into companies with radical new ideas, and then resign soon after when they don't achieve their stated goals. A culture is hard to understand, which makes it hard to define, which makes it hard to change.

The psychologist Jonathan Haidt writes that 'moral systems are interlocking sets of values, virtues, norms, practices, identities, institutions, technologies, and evolved psychological mechanisms that work together to suppress or regulate self-interest and make cooperative societies possible'. Organisations, with their technologies and processes and office locations, and their mission statements and codes of practice and people, are moral systems. It's important to acknowledge this, because when you take on culture change you are essentially attempting to break, or at least reboot, a moral system. Culture is a moral system, and messing with someone's moral code is taboo.

Stack's insight was to try to make the rules clear and the playing field level from the moment you start working for Springfield Remanufacturing (SRC). With the Employee Stock Ownership Plan, everyone has an opportunity to share in the possible rewards of a growing company but they have to shoulder some of the risk. The more risk you individually take on, the more you stand to benefit; and equally, if SRC collectively makes bad decisions everyone suffers proportionally as a result. In a low-margin business like remanufacturing, the impetus is to take a long-term view and work together to make consistently good decisions.

Jack Stack was fortunate in the sense that his opportunity to enact change came during a moment of crisis and rebirth. But what should you do if you're not presented with quite the same clear-cut need-for-change scenario, or you don't have quite the same owner-operator decision-making power?

The answer to that question is the focus of this book.

WHAT DOES AMERICAN CONSERVATISM HAVE TO DO WITH THIS?

In any documentary or dramatisation about American politics there's likely to be a meeting in an underground car park between an anonymous man and the hero of the story. It's a nod to Deep Throat, the source who provided evidence to investigative journalist Bob Woodward of Richard Nixon's involvement in the Watergate scandal. It's also meant to convey a generally accepted truth about American politics: it's cutthroat and shady, and its wheels are well greased with money.

BBC journalist Andrew Neil got his own Deep Throat moment in the 2010 documentary *Tea Party America*. Interviewing a Washington lobbyist, Neil questioned his anonymous source about the 'big money' behind the Tea Party, a conservative grassroots movement in the US that sprang up in the wake of Barack Obama's election as President in 2008 and denounced Obama and his policies as socialist. Here's part of the transcript for Neil's interview:

Neil: *Where's the big money coming from?*

Source: *For the Tea Party? Generally wealthy individuals who believe it's a just cause. There are people who are spending millions.*

Neil: *Did it start with the big money or has the big money jumped onto a grassroots bandwagon?*

Source: *The big money followed the organisation. This was an organic movement that attracted investors if you want to call them that, and the investors are here to make sure the movement succeeds and they can piggyback on that movement.*

I'm a sucker for a good political thriller and this was my 'in'. The Tea Party seemed like such a colourful and crazy bunch, and the idea that rich donors might be using them as a Trojan horse for their own ends was pretty enthralling. I started reading about conservative American politics and began learning about a world I'd previously had little reason to understand. I felt a bit like an archaeologist, brushing away the sand to eventually uncover an enormous, longstanding edifice that had been hidden from view. The more I read about American conservatism the more I began to see it as a coherent moral system, sometimes purely ideological but oftentimes politically pragmatic. And yet the question I kept coming back to was: how is it that so many middle class people can be duped, time and again by very rich people, into voting seemingly against their self-interest?

The answer to that question, I've discovered, is that people vote for their culture. That means that they vote for people who they think are like them, with similar beliefs and values, to legislate and govern to preserve and progress that culture. Today, 35% of Americans identify as conservative, in comparison to 35% who identify as moderate and 26% who identify as liberal. Republicans have been President for ten of the seventeen terms since the mid 20th century, in comparison to seven terms for Democrats. Since the 1970s, the Supreme Court has leaned consistently conservative in its judgements. There has also been a tendency, since the 1960s, for Americans to describe themselves as more conservative than their policy preferences suggest. Conservatism *as a culture* is growing.

Eventually, I realised that my question about people being duped to vote against their self-interest was simplistic. Indeed, it was the wrong question to ask. My 'aha' moment came when I realised that what has happened over the past 70 years is perhaps the greatest modern example of culture change in the Western world. The right question to ask is: how did America become so conservative?

THE RISE OF AMERICAN CONSERVATISM

The United States emerged from World War II a superpower. With its allies it had vanquished global fascism. Black and white footage of GIs returning home to the US, packed onto the decks of an ocean liner while women and children smile and wave handkerchiefs from the shore, capture the giddy relief and jubilant sense of victory of the time. In 1945 'conservatism' wasn't a popular word in America. Conservative fringe groups were accused of being un-American: liberalism, it was argued, was the only American tradition. Conservatism was simply a treacherously exotic European import.

Nevertheless, three different strands of conservative thought began to take shape in the post-war period:

1. Libertarianism: popular with captains of private industry who wanted to limit government spending, eliminate regulation of industry and significantly cut taxes.
2. Traditionalism: advanced by intellectuals who were shocked by the development of a secular society defined by mass consumption and rootlessness.
3. Anti-communism: shaped by ex-Leftist radicals who believed the West was locked in a life-or-death struggle with an adversary that sought to conquer the world.

Each strand would evolve and mutate over the next fifty years:

- Libertarians favoured economic deregulation, subscribing to the theories of the 'Chicago School' of economics. During the 1980s these ideas became known as 'supply side economics'; leading supply-sider Milton Friedman was a consultant to Ronald Reagan and Margaret Thatcher, and his influence led to the nomination of Alan Greenspan as Chairman of the Federal Reserve (the American central bank). From the vantage point of the 21st century, libertarian ideas have had the most consistent mainstream influence of all conservative movements.
- Traditionalists morphed slowly but surely into the social conservative movement. With the growth of evangelical Christianity they became the Religious Right in the 1980s under the auspices of organisations

such as the Moral Majority, led by Jerry Falwell, and the Family Research Council, founded by James Dobson. Today, social conservative positions on abortion, same-sex marriage and inter-faith relations seem anachronistic to most Americans, although the rising importance of the Hispanic and Muslim vote has helped sustain support for these issues. Social and religious conservatives are still an important voting bloc but with a diminishing influence over the mainstream.

- The anti-communists became the neoconservatives, whose hawkish, interventionist foreign policy views reigned supreme during the presidency of George W. Bush in the early 2000s. Jewish thinkers such as Irving Kristol, Leo Strauss and Norman Podhoretz exerted significant influence over key Bush Jr. administration officials such as Dick Cheney and Donald Rumsfeld, as well as provocateurs like Newt Gingrich. In these hugely partisan times, neoconservatives are a throwback to yesteryear – centrists who advocate that the US should continue to play a strong role in global affairs. Nevertheless, the spirit of anti-communism is alight in Donald Trump's America First isolationism and 'China as evil empire' outlook.

Post-war conservatives were first united by senator Barry Goldwater's 1964 run for president. Goldwater was outspoken about his belief in self-reliance and limited government, and controversially suggested that nuclear weapons could be used to prevent the spread of communism. Counter to his personal beliefs about racial equality, Goldwater opposed the Civil Rights Act of 1964 on the grounds that it was a federal intrusion on the rights of individual states to decide how to govern themselves. Branded an extremist, Goldwater lost the election in a landslide, winning only his home state of Arizona and the Deep South. His legacy was the language of rebellion and righteous fury. Generations of conservatives have used this to their advantage ever since. The influential conservative columnist George Will later wrote, 'Goldwater lost 44 states but won the future'.

I.1 *Barry Goldwater poster*

Goldwater's rebellious conservatism was particularly appealing to students. One student conservative explained it at the time: 'You walk around with your Goldwater button, and you feel that thrill of treason.' The seeds of conservative media, infamous today both within and outside the United States, bloomed on university campuses and found its first national voice in William Buckley Jr, an aggressive young intellectual. And that same 'thrill of treason' ignited the passions and imagination of College Republicans such as Lee Atwater and Karl Rove, who would become the most important political strategists of their time. Atwater, as he so often did, said it best: 'When I got into politics the establishment was all Democrats and I was anti-establishment. The young Democrats were all the ones running round in three-piece suits, smoking cigars and cutting deals so I said, "hell, I'm a Republican".'

There's a story that upon signing the Civil Rights bill, President Lyndon B. Johnson muttered darkly to an aide, 'Alright, we have lost the South for a generation'. True or not, it was a conservative prediction; the Democrats have never truly regained the South since. Two 'great white switches' characterised the two decades after Civil Rights: first when southern white Democrats voted heavily for Republican Richard Nixon in 1968, and later when many southern white Democrats came to identify as Republican conservatives during the Reagan years. This realignment is all the more remarkable when you consider that the South had *always* been solidly Democratic – indeed, the Ku Klux Klan formed to prevent a viable Republican Party establishing itself in the South (the Great Emancipator Abe Lincoln, who ended slavery, was a Republican). Before the great white switches, Republican electoral success was built on landslide victories in northern states that would compensate for underwhelming performances in the South. Today, Republicans have entrenched their hold on the South via strategic alliances with conservative groups. These alliances have irrevocably changed the party.

The last question that Andrew Neil asks his Deep Throat in *Tea Party America* is 'does the big money want to change the Republican Party?' It was disingenuous, because he knew the answer. The big money had more or less publicly admitted that it did. Charles and David Koch are the billionaire owners of the second largest privately owned company in the US, Koch Industries. Since the 1970s the brothers have spent hundreds of millions of dollars discreetly building the infrastructure needed to launch a conservative libertarian revolution. They inherited Koch Industries from their father, Fred, who was a founding member of the John Birch Society, a libertarian group shunned by Goldwater and dismissed by William Buckley as 'crackpot alley'. In 1995, Koch deputy Rich Fink explained their culture-change strategy to other potential investors. Likening it to the production process, Fink argued that social and political change required the development of intellectual raw materials, their conversion into specific policy products, and the marketing and distribution of these products to citizen consumers. Charles Koch admitted that their donor network of around 500 very wealthy Americans had created a 'war chest' of $889 million to spend on the 2016 presidential elections, equal to the individual amounts spent by the Republican and Democratic National Committees.

The Koch's social change strategy is a top-down method, guided by an elite. Richard Viguerie, a long-time conservative activist, describes a bottom-up approach, led by the grassroots. For mass movements to achieve power, Viguerie argues that they need:

1. a dedicated vanguard
2. self-identification as a movement
3. communication networks
4. money
5. elements of the establishment to opt to join the new order.

Fink and Viguerie were describing the same process, just from different perspectives. Strange as it may seem, elite and grassroots conservative activists have been comfortable bedfellows in their pursuit of lasting culture change. Like Jack Stack's managers and employees at SRC, they share the same worldview and have used it to their advantage. In 1996, two years before his death, Barry Goldwater lamented to Bob Dole, then running for president: 'We're the new liberals of the Republican party. Can you imagine that?' Fourteen years later, crowing over the success of Tea Party candidates in the 2010 Congressional midterm elections, conservative activist Brent Bozell proudly declared 'the moderate wing of the Republican Party is dead'.

HOW ORGANISATIONS CAN LEARN FROM THE RISE OF AMERICAN CONSERVATISM

The Tea Party's moment as the conservative vanguard passed, but this vanguard reared its head again with the election of Donald Trump as president. Conservatism has effectively transformed itself from an obscure fringe movement into one of the most powerful political forces in the

United States. There is a lot that organisations and leaders that want to effect sustainable culture change can learn from this.

This book is structured to make these lessons clear. Culture change is a complicated task, and American conservatism is a complex subject. So, I've organised the book into three parts, each addressing an important aspect of organisational change:

Part I: **People change** – with a focus on employees, customers and other stakeholders

Part II: **Communicating change** – with a focus on communication styles and formats

Part III: **Leading change** – with a focus on management and implementation

There are also three storylines running through the book, each about a different aspect of conservatism:

Storyline 1: Conservative business – with a focus on the tobacco industry

Storyline 2: The conservative movement – with a focus on activism and the media

Storyline 3: Conservative politics – with a focus on campaign strategy and governance

Each storyline features once in each of the three parts, which gives us nine 'case stories'. Each case story is a historical narrative about American conservatism with a clear lesson about organisational culture change. In fact, with my tongue somewhat in cheek, I've called each of these lessons 'commandments', so that there are Nine Commandments about culture change that serve as a checklist of things to ensure you do when you embark on a culture-change mission. Each case story is structured in the same way, starting with the historical narrative and ending with a section that explains in more detail how the lesson can be applied within an organisation as part of a change programme.

PART I: PEOPLE CHANGE

Case Story	Title	Commandment
1	Marlboro	Use data and your gut to segment your people into employee persona types.
2	Suburbia	Understand the world your people live in and how their responsibilities influence their hopes and fears.
3	Personas	People are groupish so be part of the group.

PART II: COMMUNICATING CHANGE

Case Story	Title	Commandment
4	Freedom	Ground your change vision in heritage and history, and lead with a promise to take your people 'back to the future'.
5	Entertainment	Use the principles of entertainment to educate and engage people in service of your change vision.
6	Channels	Use your communications channels inventively to keep people focused on achieving your change vision.

PART III: LEADING CHANGE

Case Story	Title	Commandment
7	Misfits	Build a change team of people who understand both the cultural surface and its deeps, and who have the skills and behaviours needed to change it.
8	Networks	Cultivate and use your networks at all levels of your organisation and industry, without letting them co-opt or derail your change plan.
9	Trump	Apply all the commandments I've given so far to find your X Factor, which will make the impact of your change efforts greater than their sum.

No book about American conservatism can avoid the topic of race, and race relations and the treatment of racial difference by conservatives are a topic that I cover frequently throughout the book. There's nothing of substance though about the so-called Alt Right, or the Ku Klux Klan, or any other overtly white supremacist organisation. White supremacist organisations in the United States are, frankly and thankfully, poorly organised and led, with low membership numbers and incoherent philosophies. There's nothing of value that we can learn from these groups.

PART I
People change

Marlboro

Commandment

Use data and your gut to segment your people into employee persona types.

This story starts with Steve Jobs – perhaps a libertarian, but for most people the antithesis of conservatism. For someone who was focused so intently on the future, it was curious that Jobs chose to speak entirely about the past in his commencement speech to the Class of 2005 at Stanford University. It's likely the previous year's diagnosis of pancreatic cancer still loomed heavy in his mind, despite the reprieve he'd been given by his doctors almost immediately after the diagnosis when a biopsy showed it was operable. Perhaps it was a foreboding of the relapse that would take his life just six years later.

> When I was young, there was an amazing publication called *The Whole Earth Catalog*, which was one of the bibles of my generation … On the back cover of their final issue was a photograph of an early morning country road, the kind you might find yourself hitchhiking on if you were so adventurous. Beneath it were the words: 'Stay hungry. Stay foolish.' It was their farewell message as they signed off. Stay hungry. Stay foolish. And I have always wished that for myself. And now, as you graduate to begin anew, I wish that for you.

The hitchhiker allusion was deliberate. Its creator, Stewart Brand, later recounted how the idea came to him:

The image I had in my mind was of a hitchhiker at dawn on a road somewhere and the sun comes up and there are trains going by. The frame of mind of the young hitchhiker is one of the freest frames of mind there is. You're always a little bit hungry and you know you are being completely foolish.

You don't have to have read *The Whole Earth Catalog* (I haven't), nor be nostalgic for the world it came from, to appreciate the power of that image and those words. As art, for the sentiment it expresses, and as advertising for the way it enshrined the Whole Earth legacy, it's a wonderful piece of work. Look at it. Maybe instead of a hitchhiker, imagine being a cowboy. Tell me it doesn't look like an advert for Marlboro.

Most people who have lived on planet Earth long enough to know what Apple is have heard of the Marlboro Man. Even those who are too young to remember the ads on TV or in magazines know what Marlboro Country is. While smoking has fallen out of fashion in the West, Marlboro is still rightly remembered as one of the 20th century's most brilliant brand creations. As a long-running advertising campaign it has had lasting resonance – since 1972 Marlboro has been the world's most popular cigarette.

The story of Marlboro can teach us a lot about the importance of understanding people in order to motivate them to change their behaviour. A brand that began as an unpopular cigarette for women took on a life of its own, beyond the product it represented, by tapping into the same powerful notions of identity as *The Whole Earth Catalog*'s final message that so captivated Steve Jobs. It wasn't a creative accident; rather, it was a brand that was developed by learning from years of investigation by the tobacco industry into what makes people hungry and foolish. And, indeed, conservative. The Marlboro Man, unlike *The Whole Earth Catalog*, was unashamedly a conservative hero whose appeal transcended political leanings.

In the same Stanford commencement speech, Jobs also said 'in life, you have to trust your gut'. I'm paraphrasing slightly, but it is absolutely true for understanding people and how best to help them change. Reliable gut feelings are

1.1 *The Whole Earth Catalog*

based on familiarity with particular situations, and experienced executives and managers will be very familiar with the ways in which employees behave in different situations, when morale is high and when it is low. Most organisations have a lot of different data on file about their employees, and that data is a good place to start in trying to understand them demographically. But to truly understand a body of people as both a single culture and a series of subcultures you're going to have to use your gut.

So, the commandment for this case story is: Use data and your gut to segment your people into employee persona types.

THE SECRETS OF SEGMENTATION

At the beginning of the 20th century the cigarette was taboo, indulged only by effeminate, bohemian men and eccentric upper-class women. World War I and the Jazz Age changed that. Camaraderie in the trenches was expressed with the sharing of a cigarette, and pictures of young men with cigarettes dangling from their lips captured the power of the human spirit amidst the appalling bloodshed of the Great War. As the war ended the American Century began, banishing forever the European notion that life was nasty, brutish and short. American modernity promised the luxuries and convenience of consumer culture and the thrill of individual independence. Recognising that women constituted 50% of any given population, advertisers employed experts from the emerging fields of psychology and public relations to overcome social objections to women smoking. This was accomplished most strikingly with the 'torches of freedom' stunt, when young women marched down Fifth Avenue in New York City smoking famously and blowing smoke in the face of traditional ideas about femininity. In a few turbulent years, the cigarette became a totem of social change. Central to this was its flexibility – its capacity to symbolise patriotism and sacrifice at the same time as it represented sophistication and progressiveness.

All this helped the tobacco industry grow enormously. By the mid 20th century, cigarettes accounted for 1.4% of the US gross national product and 3.5% of consumer spending on nondurable goods. Yet for all its symbolic power, the cigarette was a commodity. Despite research and development efforts to find unique ways of curing and treating tobacco, blind tests showed time and again that smokers found it impossible to discern their brand from the next. In a fiercely competitive industry, the challenge was to create cigarette brands that commanded consumer loyalty better than other brands. Later, when the link between smoking and disease was scientifically established, it became necessary to make a brand more nuanced in the way it communicated the subtle pleasures of smoking to those who wanted to give up or cut back. Commensurate with the industry's growth, tobacco companies began to spend billions of dollars each year researching consumer behaviour, with the goal of converting 'pre-smokers' to 'starters', persuading smokers of competitor brands to switch, and reassuring 'quitters' that smoking lights or filtered versions of the brand was better than stopping altogether. All of this had to be done without alienating hardcore 'enjoyers' who were still committed to a brand's full-flavour cigarette.

Earlier than most industries, Big Tobacco came to understand that its customer segmentation had to work in three dimensions:

1-D: length of experience as a smoker
2-D: depth of commitment to the habit
3-D: self-identity in terms of preferred cigarette brand.

A brand, accordingly, could not be just a visual image. It would need to be a world into which a smoker was tempted and in which they could be convinced to stay. To design an effective brand world, tobacco marketers needed to understand three things, each related to the dimensions of segmentation:

1. why people start smoking
2. why they keep smoking
3. how they select a cigarette brand.

Scientists could explain in part why people *keep* smoking: the flue-curing method of preparing the 'bright' tobacco that was used in cigarettes made their smoke alkaline, which, unlike pipe or cigar smoke, made it possible to inhale. As such, nicotine could be absorbed into the bloodstream and nicotine, it turned out, is highly addictive. Determining why people start smoking and why they choose particular brands was less easy to quantify. But it is theories that answer these two conundrums that led to the creation of Marlboro and that give us powerful insights about how to approach preparing a change campaign in an organisation.

WHY PEOPLE START SMOKING

One of the hardest things about effecting change in an organisation, especially at the outset, is generating some excitement for it. Most people in an organisation either fear being made redundant or couldn't care less about what's happening. Indifference is the most maddening and challenging (non) response. When you're involved with a change programme and you can't get people to comment on your internal communications or ask interested questions at 'town hall' meetings or sign up to be 'change ambassadors', it feels a bit like unrequited love. You take it to heart – what's wrong with me, why won't they even *glance* at me?

I've been in this situation a few times. During one of them, I read Malcolm Gladwell's bestseller *The Tipping Point*. Gladwell popularised the notion of 'stickiness' – the ways in which trends catch on. Aspects of *The Tipping Point* have come in for criticism in recent years, but its case study on teenage smoking is truly insightful. When I first read it all those years ago I knew in my gut that what he wrote about smoking was true, and it revealed to me why no one gave a shit about our change campaign.

In an effort to understand more about why teenagers smoke, Gladwell sent a questionnaire to several hundred people asking them about their earliest experiences with cigarettes. The responses he printed have a kind of lyrical beauty to them. Here are a few:

> My mother smoked … and when she smoked she looked so elegant and devil-may-care that there was no question that I'd smoke someday. She thought people who didn't smoke were kind of gutless.

The first kid I knew who smoked was Billy G ... He was the first kid to date girls, smoke cigarettes and pot, drink hard alcohol and listen to druggy music ... The draw for me was the badness of it, and the adult-ness, and the way it proved the idea that you could be more than one thing at once.

The first person who I remember smoking was a girl named Pam P ... We used to sit in the back of the bus and blow smoke out the window. She taught me how to inhale, how to tie a man-tailored shirt at the waist to look cool, and how to wear lipstick. She had a leather jacket. Her father was rarely home.

Gladwell wrote that there is a certain type of personality who initiates other people into smoking. To sociologists, they exhibit traits like sociability, rebelliousness, sexual impulsiveness, honesty, indifference to the opinions of others, risk-taking and thrill seeking (interestingly, traits that, in the extreme, are associated with psychopathy). To the layperson, these people just seem exciting. Gladwell's summary is what rocked me though:

Smoking was never cool. *Smokers* are cool.

Tobacco isn't sugar, and no one likes the taste of their first cigarette. Everyone's first suck-cough-and-splutter puts paid to the idea that smoking in and of itself is cool. Like a good game, smoking at the outset is a form of hard work that we choose for ourselves. Rookie smokers persevere because they sense that, when they finally *get it*, they won't just look cool, they'll actually *be* cool, like the person who first taught them how to do it (accordingly, the tobacco industry developed a technique they interchangeably called influential seeding and (before the internet was a thing) viral advertising, where 'cool people' would be paid to smoke in bars and clubs frequented by students and young people).

Starting to smoke is a way of proving to ourselves that we *can* change and signalling to others that we *have* changed. If smoking is, eventually, addictive, the ritual of starting to smoke is a kind of social contagion.

1.2 *The spark of romance*

HOW PEOPLE SELECT A CIGARETTE BRAND

As the case against cigarettes gathered pace in the 1990s, a French Professor at Cornell University wrote a maudlin elegy to the habit he, like so many other smokers, loved but knew he should quit. In *Cigarettes Are Sublime*, Richard Klein rhapsodises:

> A cigarette bespeaks the smoker, as the poem the poet … The cigarette is analogous to what linguists call a shifter, like the word *I* … The smoker manipulates the cigarette, like the word I, to tell stories to herself about herself – or to another.

If the cigarette as commodity was a totem of social change, the cigarette in context – in a person's hand as they gesture or their mouth as they pout – is a form of self-expression. And as the advertising supremo Leo Burnett remarked at a time when more than 40% of Americans smoked, 'outside the clothes and jewellery you wear, a cigarette package is your most frequently exposed possession'. A cigarette brand was fundamentally part of someone's identity.

The title of Klein's book, facetious though it seems, speaks to the ways in which humans project contradictory desires onto the products we buy. Seeking to explain why people love things that taste nasty and make us sick, Klein found an answer in the German philosopher Immanuel Kant's definition of 'sublime': 'the sublime, as distinct from the merely beautiful, affords a negative pleasure because it is accompanied … by a moment of pain'. It follows that the way people choose a brand for a sublime habit is equally paradoxical. In choosing a particular brand of cigarette, would-be smokers and 'switchers' are pushed and pulled by three forms of cognitive dissonance:

1. People are neophilic and neophobic. They want new things but are afraid of things that are too unfamiliar.
2. People are groupish and individualistic. They want to be accepted as members of particular social groups, yet be unique and different to others.
3. People want to be sheep and wolves. They want to be known for their traditional manners and classic tastes, as well as for being unpredictable and cutting edge.

Claude E. Teague, R.J. Reynolds Tobacco's Assistant Chief of R&D in the 1970s, made something of a name for himself as an expert in youth smoking. In response to the neophilic vs neophobic challenge, Teague recommended searching through American history textbooks to find brand names and images that would resonate with young people. He addressed the groupish vs individualistic and sheep vs wolves dilemmas in a 1973 memo:

If the desire to be daring is part of the motivation to start smoking, the alleged risk of smoking may actually make smoking attractive. If the 'older' establishment is preaching against smoking, the anti-establishment sentiment would cause the young to be defiant and smoke. Thus, a new brand aimed at the young group should not in any way be promoted as a 'health' brand, and perhaps should carry some implied risk.

A study from the 1990s confirmed that some smokers explained their choice of cigarette brand as a process of elimination, selecting one brand because they didn't like the types of people who smoked another brand. In response to the question 'If [a cigarette brand you don't smoke] were a woman, what kind of woman would that be?' Newport smokers characterised smokers of Marlboro Lights as 'white girls who have to look perfect all the time', while smokers of Marlboro Lights regarded Newport smokers as 'slutty girls' who 'think they're tough' but are really 'immature and ignorant'.

A template for creating new brands emerged as the tobacco companies' knowledge and understanding of how people selected cigarette brands improved.

A brand name and associated image would be chosen for its resonance in specific geographical markets, from the Virgin Mary in the Philippines, to Shakespeare's Hamlet in the UK, to Red Star in North Korea and the Taj Mahal in India.

The target audience in that geographical market would be segmented both demographically (by social group) and psychographically (according to personal values, attitudes and lifestyle choices). Examples, in the industry's own words, include:

Demographics	Psychographics
Women	Affluent extroverts
Blacks	Slackers and drifters
Jews	Rockers and punkers
The homeless	Preps and goody-goodies
Blue-collar workers	New traditionalist nesters
Military personnel	Upscale intellectuals
LGBT	Middle tar downshifters
Physicians, nurses and hospital workers	Slobs and burnouts
The elderly	Aspiring sophisticates

From there, a sales strategy would be created that would focus on 'suggesting' the brand to the target audience, rather than forcing it on them. In addition to traditional advertising, suggestion was a creative effort could that involve, for example, sponsoring a competition for university students to name a new cigarette filter (Brown & Williamson in 1955), launching a new music talent campaign (Philip Morris in 1989) or writing advertorials like the weekly Kent Sports Business Column in the *Wall Street Journal*, which created an editorial space to promote the Kent family of cigarettes (Lorillard in 1982).

By the 1950s, the cigarette industry had half a century's experience of how to segment markets and design brand worlds that appealed to new and experienced smokers as well as dedicated and wavering smokers. Philip Morris and the creative agencies they worked with showed how powerful this knowledge could be when they took the risk of reimagining Marlboro. In so doing they rewrote the playbook for consumer brand design and marketing.

WELCOME TO MARLBORO COUNTRY

Science is slow and conscientious. The link between cigarette smoke and lung cancer was not proven conclusively with a smoking-gun study; instead, research by a number of scientists in the late 1940s and early 1950s advanced the unpleasant idea in the public conscious, a little like a poisonous gas noxiously filling a sealed room. At this time, Philip Morris was the smallest of the six major cigarette manufacturers in the United States and without a product in the top five selling brands. Their goal was to create a brand with mass-market appeal that could challenge the dominance of the top three brands: Camel, Lucky Strike and Chesterfield. Each of the top three was, in its own way, associated with progressive America – urban, carefree and youthful. Each was an unfiltered cigarette. As Americans increasingly began to doubt the safety of a national habit, Philip Morris wanted to introduce a reassuring brand that they could argue was a safer smoke. Marlboro, a premium filtered brand for women, was chosen for a macho makeover, with the rationale that a more masculine image might alleviate fears that smoking could kill. If consumers identified with an invincible strongman, they might themselves become resistant to disease.

Philip Morris' then PR director, George Weissman, put together a crack team of external public opinion experts, marketers and packaging manufacturers to make Marlboro attractive to two target audiences: men who wanted an adventurous life away from the nine-to-five, and women who fantasised about the raw sexuality of such rugged masculinity. Consumer research quickly raised a problem though – filter tips were considered 'sissyish' by these audiences. So, Weissman contracted a British manufacturer to design a highly durable, crush-proof cardboard flip-top carton, similar to one that his production chief, Clark Ames, had discovered was popular in Germany. Weissman also hired Louis Cheskin, whose 'sensation transference' theory argued that consumer brand choice was influenced primarily by packaging aesthetics and the power of colour. Building on Cheskin's research, the design firm Frank Gianninoto & Associates developed the Marlboro crest, which signified quality and prestige, and recommended bold red accents for both functional reasons (strong visibility on the shelves) and emotional ones (denoting festivity and bold enjoyment). The sturdy package and its striking design countered the wimpy connotations of filter tips. Finally, Weissman chose to work with the Leo Burnett agency to design Marlboro's go-to-market strategy.

Unlike most advertising agencies that were based on and around Madison Avenue in New York City, the Leo Burnett agency was headquartered in Chicago. Founder Leo Burnett had a reputation for fashioning romantic visions of the American heartland in his creative work, influenced by his conservative upbringing:

In the Michigan town where I was raised you could hear the corn growing on hot nights. I snuck up on Chicago, slowly, by way of outlying cities. When I finally got there I was 40 years old and confirmed in my colloquial ways.

Competitors criticised Burnett's creative work as unsophisticated and 'almost childish', but he won the Marlboro account because of his deep-rooted affiliation for Middle America. With cigarette ash sprinkled on his waistcoat and lapels, Burnett would flip through his folder of 'Corny Language' at his desk and let intuition guide his branding decisions. His legacy was an understanding that the richest source for advertising and branding ideas was the roots of culture – in history, mythology and folklore.

Led by Draper Daniels, Leo Burnett's Creative Director (and the man on whom *Mad Men*'s Don Draper is based), the creative team approached the Marlboro account with a question as curt as the image they were trying to sell: 'what's the best masculine image in the US today?' Bizarrely, the early frontrunner was a cab driver, until Leo himself whipped out a magazine with a cowboy on the cover and declared 'the cowboy is an almost universal symbol of admired masculinity'. Burnett's gut instinct proved correct – of all the archetypes they tested, the cowboy proved the most successful with the public and sales jumped by 3,241% in 1955 when the first ads rolled out. Even so, it would take a decade of trial and error to truly discover Marlboro Country.

Decades later, John Benson, a former account executive for Leo Burnett, would say that the Marlboro cowboy 'dispels the myth that in order to attract young people you've got to show young people'. From the get-go, Marlboro used older male models in Marlboro ads, but the earliest were 'Hollywood cowboys' in static poses wearing costumes and obviously fake tattoos on their hands. Moreover, the Marlboro Man of old had to explain himself: 'I'm a rancher. Grew up in this part of the country. Own my own ranch, ride from one end of it to the other every day. I like the life a man leads out here, the good feeling of being your own boss.' The message was right but the details were not. Philip Morris and the Leo Burnett team soon realised that they would have to do something more authentic to achieve the stratospheric success for which they hoped.

Thirteen years after the birth of the Marlboro Man, Draper Daniels and his team found what they were looking for. Thirty-eight-year-old Darrell Winfield, raised in California by dustbowl 'Okies', was a working cowboy on a ranch in Wyoming. Though he 'scared the hell' out of the team, they also agreed he looked like a 'born leader, without enemies'. Winfield became the most-used model from a team of four real cowboys who portrayed Marlboro Men in the brand's golden era of advertising, from the late 1960s to the late 1980s. Brand rules as complex as the Marlboro world was simple were created to guide photographers and marketers. The Leo Burnett team set out to chronicle the modern American West, telling timeless stories with visual vignettes about what a cowboy does. The focus, always, was on emotion – using the background of western states, from Montana down to Texas, to communicate the myth of the free spirit, and natural lighting to emphasise sharp masculine angles. Looking back, Marlboro photographer Norm Clasen marvelled at what they achieved:

> The Marlboro campaign was so powerful, so recognisable that at one point there was a double page spread in *Life* magazine; it was a photograph of Darrell with rain dripping off his hat, his slicker on, and he's in a barn lighting a cigarette. They ran it with no type whatsoever and they had a 90-something percent recognition rate, which is unheard of in the advertising industry.

By the time Marlboro became the world's bestselling cigarette brand, Camel had fallen down the rankings. Nevertheless, the two brands remained arch enemies of a sort and their respective parent companies continually defined the two brands in direct opposition to one another. In a brand persona comparison from the early 1990s, Philip Morris described the Marlboro Man as 'old fashioned' and 'Mr Right', in stark contrast to Joe Camel who was 'spontaneous' and 'Mr Tonight'. To drive home the point that the Marlboro Man was a conservative hero and Joe Camel a liberal gadfly, they identified actor-celebrities who embodied each: left-wing libertines such as Jack Nicholson, Warren Beatty and Mick Jagger for Joe Camel, and

right-wing hard cases such as John Wayne, Clint Eastwood and Chuck
Norris for the Marlboro Man.

Though the Marlboro Man couldn't, in the end, protect his smokers
from the threat or ravages of smoke-related disease, his brand of classic American conservatism proved to have greater longevity than Joe

1.3 *The classic flip-top packet*

Camel's cartoonish coolness. In that sense, Camel overreached, proving so immensely popular with very young children that R.J. Reynolds were forced to retire him in 1997, under pressure from public interest groups and the American Congress. The Marlboro Man, of course, eventually went the same way, but today the campaign is remembered primarily for the lifestyle marketing trend it pioneered: a heroic image of a person who the consumer aspires to be like, or already imagines he or she is.

What can we learn from Case story 1?

The singer Tom Waits once said of song-writing: 'how do you take a photo of your driveway and make it look like the road of life?' It's a question about connecting personal creative output to universal themes so that it appeals to a wide variety of people. Tobacco is a product of the rural, conservative south, but cigarette brands are created by ad agencies in the urban, liberal north. It's telling that the most successful brand tells a timeless tale of the mythic West. Marlboro was an experiment to attract people with very different worldviews away from their current choice of cigarette by putting a visual story to the feeling of smoking a cigarette. The strapline for that story might be: 'when I smoke I feel American'.

Think for a second about just how powerful that statement is. Human memory is associative, referencing past experiences and knowledge to make sense of the here and now. Because our memories have finite capacity, we organise ideas into mental categories to help remember what they mean. Accordingly, single words and phrases are imbued with a kaleidoscopic range of associations – ambiguous, random, multi-sensory. 'Smoking' and 'American' are two such words.

The nature of our memories makes us creative but illogical creatures. It stands to reason that the more we understand other people and their personal circumstances and worldviews, the better we'll be able to influence them. Marketing is obviously built around this, and the success of Marlboro is testament to all that the tobacco industry was learning about consumer psychology and behaviour. Why then don't organisations apply the same logic to their change programmes?

Early in Case story 1 I mentioned a failing change campaign I was working on. It was failing because the change we were selling didn't seem particularly exciting or fulfilling for those who would be affected by it. Without thinking much about our people and their motivations, we were asking them to help the organisation change without dangling the prospect of the opportunity for *personal* change and the feelings of fulfilment that personal change brings.

Based on the lessons from this case story, here's how I'd do things differently.

Large organisations face the same challenge as Marlboro when it comes to understanding their people. They're diverse places full of people with different cultural backgrounds from different generations with different job responsibilities. They're full of different personality types with different motivations and ambitions. Every single one of them is contradictory and complicated. Nevertheless, there is a common culture across every organisation – or, at the very least, across a particular office or business unit.

First, I'd want to define that culture. I'd start by writing down what I think the culture is, based on my own observations. I'd then canvas others, asking them to write down how they see it, with the aim of agreeing on a definition.

Next, I'd want to segment my audience – those people who will be affected by and involved in the change programme. Like the tobacco companies, I'd use guidelines to help me build some three-dimensional audience personas:

1-D: length of service at the organisation
2-D: depth of commitment to the organisation
3-D: motivations for working for the organisation.

I'd also use a selection of the vast amounts of data that large organisations can access to inform the development of those personas:

- on employment status, demographic data and remuneration;
- responses to employee surveys about how people feel about the organisation's strategic goals and as a place to work;

- from internal sources, such as how managers view the skills and attitudes of the people in their teams, and how those people view their managers;
- from external sources like glassdoor.co.uk where people share their (usually anonymous) opinions about what it's like to work for the organisation;
- from marketing materials and brand analysis, which reflect, in part, organisational and industry culture.

Finally, I'd think about commonalties across each of those personas in relation to the organisation's culture. Specifically, I'd focus on:

1. Where there's a choice, why do people work for this organisation rather than a competitor or the company next door?
2. What do people commonly think would make the organisation better, in terms of as a place to work as well as in its strategic goals?

In answering those two questions I'd be hoping to understand how people emotionally connect to the organisation's mission and vision, and the reality of working there. In thinking about how I might begin to build a change campaign, I'd once again look to lessons from Marlboro and be asking:

- Who is someone who works for the organisation that a majority of people think is cool? Why are they cool – what is their appeal?
- What tangible thing – a product or system or method that's unique to the organisation – is a totem that reflects the reasons the organisation exists?
- What symbols, phrases and visual concepts, specific to the industry or organisational culture, have a 'heroic' association?

In *The Leo Burnett Book of Advertising*, a kind of insider's guide to the world of advertising that served as a promotional pamphlet for the agency itself, author Simon Broadbent wrote:

Somewhere in every product are the seeds of a drama which best expresses that product's value to a consumer. The secret of effective advertising is not the creation of new words and pictures, but of putting words and pictures into new relationships.

This statement can be rewritten as a mantra for designing organisational change programmes:

Somewhere in every organisation are the seeds of a drama which best expresses that organisation's value to its employees. The secret of effective change is not rational explanations that justify new organisational structures and processes, but of understanding why that drama motivates people so it can be used to get people excited about change.

Suburbia

Commandment

Understand the world your people live in and how their responsibilities influence their hopes and fears.

The bartender in the Nugget Casino in Fallon, Nevada was high on meth and said she'd give me a good deal: a beer for free if I gave her a good tip and fuck what the house thought.

I shrugged. 'Works for me. What's the better route to southern California: Highway 50 or Highway 95?'

The Nugget was extremely dark and empty. 'Nuthin' down 95. Never been to California so I dunno.'

The slot machines were crowded very closely together and the air conditioning exacerbated the overwhelming smell of stale cigarette smoke. Fifty miles back up the road my wife and I had driven past Lovelock Correctional Center, home at the time to OJ Simpson. We agreed that we might as well see a bit more of Nevada's outlaw country and chose the left-hand path, Highway 95.

Fallon, pop. 8,606, is at the crossroads of Routes 50 and 95. The Nevada portion of Route 50 is nicknamed the Loneliest Highway in America because of the desolate terrain it covers. Driving west, once you're in California, Route 395 takes you south down the eastern flank of the Sierra Nevada mountain range, a stunningly beautiful drive that justifies 395's 'scenic highway' designation. Highway 95, running parallel to 395, is just as desolate as Highway 50, drifting across arid desert valleys between distant mountain ranges on its run down to Las Vegas. Admittedly, Route 95 was an odd choice of road to take.

Nevada is famous for its ghost towns that were abandoned when the silver ran dry, but it's more interesting for the half-dead outposts of civilisation that are spread infrequently down Route 95. We made a habit of stopping at the roadside, next to threadbare gas stations and diners, to explore abandoned motels, frozen in time in sepia-tone 1970s furnishings, and burnt-out wooden houses littered with rattlesnake skins and children's toys. In a shack in Mina, it struck me why prostitution, gambling and tax avoidance are legal in Nevada: it lies in the shadow of California, a state with an abundance of everything. Nevada, with as little to offer as California has a lot, does what it can to get by. The land is harsh and its geography unfavourable. Sometimes the government lays a road or a corporation builds a factory, and like wildflowers a mini economy will bloom. But what big government and big business sometimes provide they can just as easily take away. When roads are rerouted or factories moved offshore, the economies die, hence the abandoned motels and burnt-out houses. Nevadans, whether born and raised or just passing through, know that they can only rely on themselves for welfare and security. It's no surprise that libertarianism as a political outlook is strong in Nevada.

In the American south-west you can appreciate the appeal of the suburbs. Suburbia is a tactic in the battle for permanence against the tough American landscape and the vagaries of big government and big business. It's a methodical attempt to plant the roots of a community, by attracting people with similar cultural values, which in turn should attract employers who want a steady supply of workers. In the 1970s, the suburbs spread like wildfire through the Sunbelt, the southernmost part of the United States that stretches from Florida, Georgia and the Carolinas in the east to Arizona, southern Nevada and Southern California in the west. Kevin Phillips, the Republican political strategist who coined the term, conceived of the Sun Country as America's new settlement frontier, and predicted that like frontiers of the past its politics would be nationalistic, anti-intellectual and ethnocentric. Consistently, suburban Americans chose to identify as proud

2.1 *Abandoned home, Route 95, Nevada*

homeowners, wary taxpayers and fearful school parents. The burgeoning conservative movement would learn well how to appeal to these identities via a growing network of conservative publications, organisations and political alliances that found fertile ground in Sunbelt suburbia.

The culture of present-day America was forged in the 1970s. It was a turbulent decade in which the economy shifted towards digital technologies and computing, influencing and exacerbating significant social upheaval. Today, most organisations operate in a global environment that's reminiscent of the uncertainty that America felt in the 1970s. Employees know to expect constant job change, know that they won't be guaranteed a great pension, know that redundancy is always a possibility or that a decision they make could have serious consequences. Today, most employees are living closer to a boom–bust edge than they would have once expected and their behaviour reflects this; people behave more cautiously while living more speculatively. This lack of stability makes culture-change programmes harder to implement. It's essential to empathise with people and the world they inhabit if you're to take them on a journey to your organisation's version of the suburban idyll: prosperous, peaceful and nurturing.

So, the commandment for this case story is: Understand the world your people live in and how their responsibilities influence their hopes and fears.

THE CENTRE CANNOT HOLD

The 1960s weren't exactly peaceful. As the decade progressed, race riots across the United States escalated in frequency and levels of violence, peaking in 1968 with riots in 125 cities in the aftermath of the assassination of Martin Luther King. Typically the rioting was most deadly in northern cities such as Detroit (43 killed), Newark, New Jersey (26 killed) and Chicago (11 killed) that had seen a large influx of black Americans, fleeing the South, between the world wars. Alarmed by the increasing unrest, President Lyndon B. Johnson established the Kerner Commission to investigate the root causes.

Historians have a field day with LBJ, because he seemed to so absolutely embody the contradictoriness of white America's handling of racial integration. The statesman who followed his conscience and signed the Civil Rights bill was also the astonishingly uncouth Texan who knew no personal boundaries and bullied the hell out of all around him (he was famous for groping female employees, once griping that the invention of pantyhose 'ruined finger-fucking'; he also told his chauffeur, Robert Parker, 'as long as you are black, and you're gonna be black till the day you die, no one's gonna call you by your goddamn name. So no matter what you are called, nigger, you just let it roll off your back like water, and you'll make it. Just pretend you're a goddamn piece of furniture'). Grappling with his belief that it was only a truly united States that could 'overcome the crippling legacy of bigotry', Johnson staffed the Kerner Commission with moderates in the hope that their conclusions would be diplomatic.

Their report blindsided him. It was unequivocal: 'Our nation is moving toward two societies, one black, one white – separate and unequal'. More troubling for Johnson were the underlying reasons, which amounted to a total condemnation of middle-class America. Specifically, the report cited problematic police practices, inadequate housing and education, a discriminatory justice system and, perhaps most damningly, disrespectful white attitudes. It was not just the South, with its legacy of slavery, that was racist – it was the entire country.

The backlash was fierce: 53% of white Americans disagreed with the report; 58% of black Americans thought it was spot on. This discrepancy hinted at an uncomfortable truth about the gospel of American self-reliance: after Civil Rights, while most whites *accepted* racial equality they didn't much support policies designed to *reduce* racial inequality. A kind of 'here's your freedom, now go make it work for you' attitude prevailed. The Kerner Report was one of the last political artefacts of a centre-liberal America. In plainspoken language it argued just how the soul of the country was being torn apart. If drastic action were not taken, the centre ground that Civil Rights sought to win would not hold.

The writer Joan Didion used this line – 'the centre cannot hold', quoting the poet W. B. Yeats – as an epigraph in *Slouching Towards Bethlehem*, the first of her collected essays and articles about California life in the 1960s. Didion was an inversion of LBJ: cool-eyed and cold-blooded, elegant, passive-aggressive. Like LBJ, she was a bellwether for centrism, born of conservative, Old California stock in Sacramento but with strong liberal tendencies. Attracted and appalled by the extremes of the uber-liberal experiment, Didion set about chronicling the sixties counterculture. In the pages of *Bethlehem* and its follow-up, *The White Album*, she hobnobs with entertainment industry elites, slums the streets with hippie detritus, and ambulance-chases stories of middle Americans who moved to nondescript, inland suburbs to vicariously live the counterculture dream and end up killing their spouses and abusing their children.

Didion takes us through the streets of San Francisco in the Summer of Love, a tripped-out Dickensian hell where teenage runaways like Debbie and Jeff, in a bid to escape being forced to go to church and iron their clothes by their parents, are liable to get conscripted by the Fagin-like Deadeye, who's trying to set up a 'groovy religious group' called Teenage Evangelism; where pseudo-Marxist do-gooders get so high and confused they dress up in blackface and end up in a confrontation with the black people they profess to be helping; where five-year-old Susan is enrolled in 'Kindergarten High' by her mother, who's been feeding her acid for a year.

In Los Angeles, she comes face to face with the devil and ends up on the brink of a nervous breakdown.

Los Angeles was one of the few Sunbelt cities that had seen serious race rioting. In 1965 in the neighbourhood of Watts, part of the broad swathe of South Central LA that would spawn gangsta rap in the 1980s, 34 people were killed after an altercation between a black driver and the police blew up into five days of looting and burning. Later, the backlash against the Kerner Report coincided with the founding of the Los Angeles chapter of the Black Panther Party. The Panthers were an inevitable by-product of James Baldwin's maxim: 'to be black and conscious in America is to be in a constant state of rage'. The LA Panthers were recruited from South Central's Slauson Gang and particularly prone to wiling out. In the months immediately following their formation they engaged in public gunfights with the LAPD, leading to the deaths of gang members. At the same time, in the Simi Hills above the dense grid of South Central, Charles Manson was cultivating the Family that would go on a killing spree in a bid to bring racial apocalypse to a violent head.

Manson charmed his way into a music community that, under the heavy influence of mind-blowingly good drugs – marijuana and LSD, cocaine and heroin, had begun to blur the boundaries between sanity and madness, pleasure and self-destruction, even good and evil. Neil Young, one of the few artists to speak forthrightly of his encounters with Manson, explained Charlie's world: 'There were about eight girls who go around keeping house, cooking food, and making love to everyone'. In the songs from the Beatles' *White Album*, Manson was convinced that he heard prediction of a race war that would require whites to conquer blacks once and for all. In the summer of 1969, Manson aimed to light the spark. Didion recalled:

> This mystical flirtation with the idea of 'sin' – this sense that it was possible to go 'too far', and that many people were doing it – was very much with us in Los Angeles in 1968 and 1969. A demented and seductive vortical tension was building in the community.

The Manson murders – of movie star Sharon Tate and her friends, of local businessman Leno LaBianca and his wife Rosemary, and of drug dealer Gary Hinman – were terrifying acts of random violence by lost young methheads who had fallen under the spell of a psychopath who wanted to be a rock star. The Manson murders captivated the nation; prosecutor Vincent Bugliosi's account of the trials, *Helter Skelter*, remains the biggest-selling true crime book of all time. Steven Roberts, the Los Angeles bureau chief for the *New York Times*, explained the way the media presented the case to the American public: 'All the stories had a common thread – that somehow the victims had brought the murders on themselves. The attitude was: "Live freaky, die freaky"'.

Somewhere between the Manson murders, the assassinations of Martin
Luther King and Bobby Kennedy, and the increasingly violent anti-war
activism in protest against the Vietnam War, the sixties liberal dream died.
Civil Rights and the counterculture were supposed to be about celebrating
the opportunities that a newfound equality provided, particularly for black
people and women. But to many white Americans, it seemed that the women
caught in the counterculture vortex had, in their pursuit of freedom, found
their way into the clutches of some singularly predatory men, and that many
black Americans scorned equality, particularly on the terms of the dominant
culture. Fine, perhaps, if they kept themselves to themselves. But the consequences of Civil Rights and the counterculture were a threatening intrusion,
taking their children, killing cops and burning down their cities. If there was
some truth to the Kerner Report's findings it didn't justify social breakdown.

SUBURBAN SUNBELT ARCADIA

2.2 *Sunbelt suburbia, Nevada*

The post-war conservative vanguard had started to earn the grudging respect of America's intellectual elite. A milestone achievement was Russell Kirk's *The Conservative Mind*. Kirk was a traditionalist, who disliked big business, big government and organised labour for their bureaucracy and inhumanness. His big ideas against 'big' organisations held broad appeal across the political spectrum and the book was reviewed favourably. A decade earlier, Friedrich Hayek's *The Road to Serfdom* had been equally well received, arguing that classical liberal economics – the ideology on which libertarian-ism is based – was an antidote to fascism. In the mainstream, conservatism was being 'devulgarised' – the problem for the traditionalists and libertarians was that they were not natural conservative bedfellows.

The anti-communists – that third strand of conservative thought – helped bridge the gap to influence the platform of united conservatism on which Barry Goldwater would run for president in 1964. The anti-communists were the first to identify Middle America as the crucible of all that was healthy and good about the United States, and the first to move the con-servative argument out of the university and into the streets (or cornfields), lighting the spark of a crusade that would resonate with millions of every-day Americans. In the creative hands of Kirk and others, this celebration of Middle America became a fusing of cultural sentiments to pastoral land-scapes, to create a powerful vision of an American Arcadia. The backdrop was partly the South (religious, old-fashioned), partly the West (pioneering, freedom-focused) and partly the Midwest (down-to-earth, community-oriented). But the foreground subject that resonated emotionally for all three factions of conservatism was the importance of private property and home ownership.

The suburbs – residential zones that, with some imagination, could be all of these geographies at once – were a logical outcome of these converging conservative ideas. The Sunbelt covered the South entirely, half the West and the fringes of the Midwest. But its appeal for migratory whites lay in the embers of the 1960s and the revolt against authority associated with Civil Rights and the counterculture.

In the early 20th century, blacks began to move en masse from the rural south to the urban north. In 1910, 91% of the black American population of 9.8 million lived in the South and only a quarter lived in cities of more than 2,500 people. By the mid sixties, the total black population had more than doubled to 21.5 million and nearly 70% lived in urban areas. The black population outside the South had increased eleven-fold to 9.7 million. That they rarely found equal opportunity elsewhere explains why so much of the rioting occurred in northern cities. It's no coincidence that as blacks migrated north to the cities, whites migrated south to the newly forming suburbs.

The South was also changing. The heavy-duty industries of the information age, from technology manufacturers to bottling and packaging plants, had infiltrated the region, eating into the land that was once all cotton and tobacco agriculture. These industries created white-collar jobs for white people who had benefitted from a level of education denied to most blacks. By the seventies, Russell Kirk's critique of big bureaucracy was shaping into a populist conservatism that still maligned big government and big labour unions but had begun to embrace big business. In hindsight, this is easily explained. The corporate community helped maintain a quaint sort of law and order that best served their aims and that was far removed from the anarchy of the counterculture.

If the problems of the sixties were an excessive permissiveness and racial strife, suburbia became a brilliant tactic in the pursuit of social control and ordered productivity. In almost every major city in the Sunbelt, the local Chamber of Commerce worked to bring new industries to the city outskirts, so that employees could easily drive to work from outlying suburbs. Sprawling suburban developments helped achieve racial peace and social harmony because they made it possible to legally exclude undesirables, which more often than not meant urban and rural blacks. The lawful segregation of the pre-Civil Rights era – '*de jure*' segregation, or Jim Crow – could continue to be pursued, albeit surreptitiously and 'off the record' – a phenomenon called 'de facto' racism.

By definition, de facto racism is hard to prove and measure. Corporate and municipal leaders in the Sunbelt saw their planning policies as progressive for the simple fact that they encouraged a conflict-averse racial moderation. Residents of the Sunbelt suburbs learned to articulate their feelings about race through colour-blind language that emphasised the importance of meritocratic individualism, along the lines of, 'we're all equal now and so what a person achieves, regardless of the colour of their skin, is a measure of their hard work and ingenuity'. If some whites privately felt that most blacks, through their behaviour, violated these intrinsic American values, heck at least they could be contained in urban centres, far away from suburbia.

Given these patterns of migration, mass political power shifted to the sprawling metropolises of the Sunbelt. The middle-class residents of these booming suburbs became the most influential swing voters in the country, up-for-grabs by politicians who could best capture their conservative hearts and minds.

BADLANDS

America is a macho culture, and conservatives tend to prize the most masculine aspects of that culture – its competitiveness, hard work ethic and individualism. So it's fascinating that it was women who led the grassroots charge of conservative activism, spreading the gospel one suburb at a time via church meetings, newsletters, conferences and organised gatherings. Male conservative intellectuals may have found common theoretical cause in the importance of property ownership and the home, but it was women who made that common cause real. None more so than Phyllis Schlafly, whose efforts on behalf of the conservative movement in the seventies would carve a clear parting down the political centre, aligning Republicans with conservatives and Democrats with liberals in a way we instinctively understand today. Historian and journalist Rick Perlstein paid rueful tribute when he called Schlafly 'probably the best political organiser we've seen in American history'.

Phyllis Stewart was born and raised a devout Catholic in St. Louis, Missouri, where she lived for the majority of her 92 years, and where she died in 2016, not long after endorsing Donald Trump for President. She first came to prominence when, in support of Barry Goldwater, she self-published *A Choice Not an Echo*, a paranoid stream-of-consciousness that struck a chord with Middle Americans who shared her concern about the North-East liberal leanings of the establishment Republican Party. A decade later, Phyllis founded the STOP ERA campaign, the flagship movement that would make her infamous.

The Equal Rights Amendment (ERA) was a proposed change to the United States Constitution that would give equal legal rights to all Americans regardless of sex. It was endorsed by Republicans and Democrats, and by 1972 had been approved by both Houses of Congress in the federal government. The next step was ratification by the individual state legislatures. Under the Stop Taking Our Privileges (STOP) banner, Schlafly rallied support across the nation from religious housewives of all faiths, and black and white working-class women, who feared that the ERA would take away the government benefits they needed to support their children. She pulled no punches, thundering from her bully pulpit: 'We reject the anti-family goals of the Equal Rights Amendment. The American women do not want abortion. They do not want lesbian privileges. And they do not want universal childcare in the hands of the government'. By 1977, the ERA had failed to achieve ratification by the necessary 38 states to get the Constitution changed. Only five of the eighteen Sunbelt states (California, New Mexico, Texas, Colorado and Kansas) ratified the Amendment. Thanks to Schlafly's efforts, the new conservative heartland was clearly delineated.

Schlafly's life and work make me think of Mildred Pierce, the protagonist of James M. Cain's classic American noir story, who lives a remarkable life during the Great Depression, lifting her family out of hardship, only to be hampered time and again by the useless men in her life who can't see her as much beyond a housewife. With Schlafly, the men in her life were simply unremarkable in comparison to her. She was a brilliant student, a model, then (supposedly) a model wife, all of which pales in comparison to her

2.3 *Phyllis Schlafly campaigning, Washington DC*

role as a one-woman conservative dynamo. Schlafly's Achilles Heel was not men but her cause; for all her early success she was battling against the tide of history when she, in her own words, 'took on the whole feminist movement'. The word paradox is overused, but Phyllis was just that – the feminist who wasn't, who earned the enmity of Americans who couldn't make sense of her fervent social conservatism. And yet, Schlafly didn't win the ERA battle of the seventies just because she was an excellent coalition builder who typed more letters and made more phone calls than her opposition. In a strange way, out of step with the times but absolutely in context with them, Schlafly *was* pro women.

The most striking theme in Joan Didion's early work is the predatory nature of men. In her novel *Play It as It Lays*, protagonist Maria Wyeth says: 'My father advised me that life itself was a crap game: it was one of the two lessons I learned as a child. The other was that overturning a rock was apt to reveal a rattlesnake'. Didion had seen up close and personal how overturning social mores gave men a licence to brutality. In *Play It as It Lays*,

Maria is coerced into having an illegal abortion, coaxed into casual sex and frequently called a cunt as she struggles with the psychological trauma of having a child in psychiatric care. In the seventies violent crime rates doubled, and by 1980 instances of violent crime and property crime were four times as high as they had been in 1960. The number of serial killers operating in the United States increased even more dramatically, from 174 in 1960 to 534 in 1970. Though the number of people directly affected by serial killers, as a proportion of the population, is very small, there's nothing more frightening, I imagine, than the possibility that a lone, predatory male might select you, randomly, as a victim. The media at the time ran rife with stories of women and children who had been kidnapped and killed by strangers. By the 1970s, the country seemed to many Americans a much bigger, scarier place than it once was.

To me, nothing captures the zeitgeist of the time like Bruce Springsteen's 1978 album, *Darkness on the Edge of Town.* Much as the early gangsta rap of the eighties would viscerally document life in the black ghettos, *Darkness* chronicles the suburbanisation of white America and the social changes that led many working Americans to conservatism. Campaigning for Barack Obama in 2012, Springsteen introduced the song 'Land of Hope and Dreams' with a short career summary: 'For the last 30 years I've been writing songs about the distance between the American Dream and the American reality'. In the seventies, that distance would be filled with the male violence of frustration and opportunism. Inspired by film noir and country music, *Darkness* is a masterpiece of tension and release. From the pent-up aggression of 'Badlands', it's clear that the voices of its songs' characters are those of the white working man. Ragged images of classic Americana – rattlesnakes, freeways, Main Street, desert twisters and self-immolation – paint a picture of the American everyman raging against family, friends and factory work: all of the things that keep him locked in place.

In the suburbs things seemed calmer and safer than the outside Badlands (there was certainly less violent crime and property crime). For conservative leaders like Phyllis Schlafly there was a genuine fear that progressives would make a naïve decision that would give legal support to men who wanted to escape their obligations:

> One of the first things that the Equal Rights Amendment would do is to invalidate the state laws that make it the obligation of the husband to support his wife. I got fed up with the women's liberationists running down motherhood and saying that it's a menial, degrading career, and that the home is a prison for women which women should be liberated from, and brought out into this wonderful workforce.

A lot of new-born conservatives – proud homeowners, wary taxpayers, fearful school parents – agreed with her.

What can we learn from Case story 2?

A culture-change programme should take into account the different worlds that your different employee types live in. Showing that you understand the threats and associated uncertainties for people will help you build a solid foundation for your programme, generating goodwill and reducing the opportunity for would-be saboteurs to exploit paranoia and cynicism for their own gain. If you understand the opportunities that people want, you can set out a roadmap for how the programme will facilitate these opportunities and motivate sensible risk-taking. Too often, change programmes are rationalised as a response to external uncertainty for the organisation along the lines of: 'We're operating in difficult markets and so we've decided to restructure so that we can respond agilely to whatever the world throws at us'. Which basically translates as: 'You're all pawns in a game of luck, so we're gambling with your jobs in the hope that it pays off for us'. Invariably that inspires a decline in morale and the loss of belief in leadership.

In the 1970s, the United States was at a national crossroads, certain neither of what it was nor what it would or should become. Looking back, it was buffeted on both sides by two very different periods of prosperity: between a liberal idealism of the Civil Rights 1960s and a conservative idealism of the consumerist 1980s. In contrast, the seventies was a cynical decade, riven by urban unrest, social conflict and paranoia. These forces shaped America in the 1970s, and the choices Americans made in this decade shaped modern American conservatism. Yet it wasn't inevitable that the US should become a right-leaning country. Conservatism made its mainstream breakthrough in the 1970s after twenty-five years as an underground movement because its leaders understood acutely how so many Americans self-identified, and unashamedly appealed to the opportunities they wanted and the fears they harboured.

Here's how I'd apply the lessons from the conservative movement in the seventies when designing a culture-change programme.

I'd want to try and see the world from the perspective of each of the employee persona types I identified using the process outlined in Case story 1. Conducting a SITU Analysis can help you do this in a systematic way.

SITU is an acronym that stands for:

Stakeholders
Issues
Trends
Uncertainties

Where:

Stakeholders	All the people in a particular employee persona's life who are dependent on or benefit in some way from the employee's job.
Issues	The specific ways in which each stakeholder is dependent on or benefits from the employee's job.
Trends	An account of the wider trends that surround the Issues.
Uncertainties	Questions that address the unknowns related to the Issues and Trends, in terms of implications for the employee.

As a generic example, let's imagine that one of your employee persona types is Multi-Stakeholder Middle Manager. By 'multi-stakeholder' I mean that they could have a variety of dependants in their personal life:

- teenage children
- spouse in part-time work

- elderly parents
- bank
- insurer, etc.

And also dependants in their professional life:

- a team they manage
- cost-saving targets
- revenue targets, i.e. your organisation is dependent on their productivity.

By 'middle manager' I mean that they probably have an above-national-average salary but don't have much in savings. They care about the work they do and take some pride in it, but don't have the ambition to become a senior manager. Some of the issues associated with different stakeholders for the middle manager might be:

Stakeholders	Issues
Teenage children	• Financial dependence: schooling/university bills. • Status dependence: part of their identity derives from having a 'professional' parent.
Elderly parents	• Social dependence: expect their children to be able to support them when they can no longer do so themselves, perhaps by moving into their home.
Bank/insurer	• Financial dependence: monthly payments related to a mortgage, car-repayment plans etc.
Team they manage	• Professional dependence: mentoring and job training new recruits. • Social dependence: helping promising junior employees navigate the culture and find new opportunities.
Revenue targets	• Financial dependence: their long-standing relationships with steady clients help them meet revenue targets without much effort.

The trends you identify in relation to each issue should help you contextualise how the issue affects the employee, for example:

Stakeholders	Issues	Trends
Teenage children	University bills	• University fees are rising but student debt is a concern, particularly because the cost of living is rising out of proportion to entry-level salaries. • University is essential for young people who aspire to follow in the footsteps of their parents into professional careers. • Lifestyle choices of young people – sometimes positive, such as a preference for healthier food; sometimes negative, such as peer pressure via social media – increase the cost of living for students.

Finally, document the uncertainties of the immediate future surrounding the issues and trends, for example:

Stakeholders	Issues	Uncertainties
Teenage children	University bills	• Exactly how much money will I be expected to spend per semester on supporting my child at university? • Will my child be able to get a job with career prospects that justify the debt they'll get into at university, or will they continue to be dependent on me? • Will they be expecting to live at home after graduating until they get a job and attain a degree of independence?

If your change programme is top-secret, you'll probably want to conduct the SITU Analysis in private conversation with your colleagues involved with the programme, using your gut instincts to complete it. If the change programme is open knowledge, you can tactfully interview employees who fit the profile for each of the persona types to understand their stakeholders and associated issues, trends and uncertainties. You can then compile their answers to complete the SITU Analysis.

Once you've completed the SITU Analysis for a particular employee persona, assign an 'Openness to Change' score to them. You can use the following scale, or create your own:

4: welcomes change
3: cautiously open to change
2: goes with the flow but would prefer not to change
1: resistant to change.

Reflecting on your SITU Analysis for the Multi-Stakeholder Middle Manager, you may decide to award them a 2 score: goes with the flow but would prefer not to change. They have a lot of dependants and a variety of important identities in relation to these dependants. Multi-Stakeholder Middle Managers are:

- hands-on parents
- concerned children (to their own elderly parents)
- primary breadwinners
- financially stretched suburbanites, etc.

As a result, career-related change is something they just don't need right now. The thing is, your organisation is dependent on the best performing of these Multi-Stakeholder Middle Managers. They competently manage teams, sharing their knowledge of the industry and how the organisation works with more junior employees, and have important relationships with clients and/or suppliers. You need to design a change programme that helps them move to a 3 score: cautiously open to change.

Knowing that they have a lot of financial dependencies, you may give anyone who's going through the change programme the opportunity to meet with a financial advisor to help them develop a financial plan and/or the opportunity to get a larger one-off bonus during the change period if they exceed their revenue targets. Change can be difficult, and the last thing you want is for them to move down to a 1 score (resistant to change), and to begin looking for a new job or bad-mouthing the initiative to the people they have influence with at the organisation. The financial advisor perk is the kind of tangible reassurance that helps lay the solid foundation you need for the programme, generating goodwill. The larger one-off bonus is the kind of thing that gives people a clear roadmap of opportunity and encourages the maintenance of productivity levels during a period of uncertainty. Take the time to empathise with how your people see the world, because the best of them are going to be assets you need to make this change programme successful.

Personas

Commandment

People are groupish so be part of the group.

Every weekday morning, hundreds of thousands of commuters rush into downtown San Francisco from surrounding suburban cities on the Bay Area Rapid Transit (BART) train. One BART line runs south from the majority-Hispanic, blue-collar city of Richmond on the shores of San Pablo Bay in the north, via the storied intellectual climes of Berkeley; a second line travels north from the new-collar, majority-Asian city of Fremont in the South Bay; two more lines head west from the white-collar, majority-white cities of Pleasanton and Concord in the East Bay: four over-ground lines that converge on the (until recently) majority-black city of Oakland before plunging under the bay to the San Francisco peninsula.

There's a doomsday thought experiment about AI called 'grey goo' that hypothesises how voracious, self-replicating nanotechnologies of the future could, following a human programming error, exponentially duplicate until they've consumed all carbon-based life and rendered the earth a lifeless mass of silicon. Over the past fifteen years there's been a kind of grey goo-ification of the Bay Area, as tech culture has crept northwards and out from Silicon Valley. Despite their fierce diversity, the BART communities have all been grey goo-ed, manifested in fast-rising property prices, heavier traffic, more housing development and malls, and start-up-related advertising everywhere. Everywhere, that is, except West Oakland.

The four San Francisco-bound BART lines briefly emerge from under Oakland and curve towards the trans-bay tunnel, giving a gritty vista of industry, a kind of living tableau that tells the story of how America was built and, indeed, how it keeps powering on. It's a breath-taking, melancholic view – of the port and its stacked containers and the cranes that lift them; of multitudes of parallel train lines that bloom away from one another, starting their journeys across the country; of the United States Post Office and its vast yard of federal trucks; of parking lots-cum-homeless encampments beneath the freeway, and rundown clapboard houses and carless boulevards.

3.1 *Homeless camp, West Oakland, California*

Whenever I glide through West Oakland on BART I think of two things. One is more of a feeling conjured by the song 'Condition Oakland', an ode to listless urban life that ends moodily with a recording of Jack Kerouac waxing lyrical about the Bay Area of yesteryear. The other is an out-of-body speculation, where I imagine what it might take as an immigrant, newly ashore with a cash-in-hand job in West Oakland, to realise the 21st-century version of the American Dream, becoming a technology kingpin across the bay. What would that journey look like? What kind of person – their innate traits, learned behaviours and, ultimately, their shifts of character – is able to achieve this?

The presidents who spearheaded the 'great white switches' of the 1970s and 1980s, Richard Nixon and Ronald Reagan, were, essentially, two such men, who fought their way from hardscrabble childhoods to the nation's top job. Though their voting blocs were the same, they were also as different as two people could be.

Nixon was insular, intellectual and resentfully insecure. In 1962, after losing the California gubernatorial election, two years after a failed run for president, his political career seemed to be over. At his 'last press conference', the worst of his traits burst to the fore as he petulantly berated the media, telling them they'd miss him when they realised 'they didn't have Nixon to kick around anymore'. His victorious opponent, Pat Brown, commiserated: 'That's something Nixon's going to regret all his life. The press is never going to let him forget it'. Six years later, Nixon was president.

Reagan was extroverted, blithely optimistic in outlook and supremely self-confident. He talked his way into the movies, and then talked his way out of a dead-end career as a journeyman actor as his interest in politics grew. Nevertheless, though he worked hard to paint a picture of an ideal life perfectly lived, Reagan's rise was long and laboured, hampered along the way by setback after setback. He was first elected president in 1980 at 69 years old, when most people, even his most ardent backers, thought his efforts too little, too late.

American lives are so often characterised by 'second acts', and none more so than Nixon's and Reagan's. But after becoming president, their paths radically diverged. Nixon resigned in disgrace in 1974 under threat of impeachment. His political life is remembered as a cautionary tale of a man who over-reached; conservatives cast him, somewhat ambivalently, as a martyr who strayed, never quite committing to the cause. Reagan, on the other hand, is God. Conservatives now remember nostalgically that on becoming president, Reagan took his rightful place on a utopian throne of conservatism that his ghost's never given up. Today, his myth continues to precede the reality.

Why did things turn out so differently for each of them? Both were Yankees who overwhelmingly won the Sunbelt South, achieving historic landslide victories for their respective second presidential terms. In doing so, both confronted the difficult subject of race, crafting personas carefully separate from their inevitably more complex selves. One of them was simply more natural in their chosen persona. People are expert at perceiving authentic-ity, and conservative voters understood that Reagan was truly one of them. Nixon, alas, was not.

So, the commandment for this case story is: People are groupish so be part of the group.

THE INVISIBLE FOUNDING FATHER

We can't talk about Nixon, Reagan and the great white switches without first talking about George Wallace, the most 'influential loser' in American politics.

Conservative historical revisionists like to imagine that the modern con-servative movement began with Barry Goldwater's failed Republican run for president in 1964. For their part, liberal historical revisionists see tragic John F. Kennedy as the spark of modern liberalism, building from the great Democratic legacy of Franklin D. Roosevelt. These simpler versions of his-tory pretend that Republicans have always been conservatives who favour small government, unregulated markets and the traditional family, and that Democrats have always been liberals who believe government has a big role to play in managing social inequalities and that individuals should be free to live their personal lives as they please. Both versions conveniently forget about George Wallace, because he was a conservative Democrat who invented the persona of the race-baiting poor man's political populist and made a long-lasting career out of it. During his heyday other presidential hopefuls had to develop personas that appealed to Wallace's constituents without losing mainstream voters who abhorred overt racism. Accordingly, there's a little bit of Wallace at the heart of both modern conservatism and liberalism (and, incidentally, a lot of Wallace in Donald Trump).

Wallace was a four-term governor of Alabama who ran for president four times, without success. Coming of age in the rural south during the Great Depression, Wallace lived amongst the desperately poor and as a junior congressman had, according to the *Alabama Journal*'s Ray Jenkins, 'a reputation as something of a socialist'. True to his class and constituents, Wallace was an anti-elitist who backed legislation aimed at curbing the power of the rich in favour of the poor and the middle classes. He was also considered enlightened in his views about race. As a judge, at a time when calling a lawyer 'Mister' was a courtesy only extended to whites, black lawyer J. L. Chestnut recalled: 'Wallace was the first judge in Alabama to call me "Mister" in a courtroom.' But Wallace was also power hungry.

Legend has it that the itinerant Mississippi Delta blues musician Robert Johnson made a pact with the devil at a crossroads that gave him fame but took his life early at the age of twenty-seven. Wallace really *did* make such a pact after losing the Alabama gubernatorial race in 1958, crafting a belligerently racist political persona in exchange for power and generating a legacy of hurt that has forever denied him respectability. It was not an uncommon route to power in the South. Bill Clinton alluded to the peculiarities of southern politics in his eulogy to senator Robert Byrd, who died a progressive Democrat but who had begun his political life as an Exalted Cyclops in his local branch of the Ku Klux Klan. As Clinton knew well, in the South, ethical beliefs and strong moral positions were considered for suckers. 'He was a country boy from the hills and hollows of West Virginia. He was trying to get elected,' Clinton said frankly of Byrd. Wallace, running again for governor in 1962, struck the same petulant tone that Nixon did in his tirade against the media: 'You know, I tried to talk about good roads and good schools and all these things, and nobody listened. And then I began talking about niggers, and they stomped the floor.' Wallace won this race in a landslide.

Still, two years later in 1964 Wallace lost the Democratic presidential primary to Lyndon Johnson. Raised to be suspicious of Republicans, he nevertheless approached Barry Goldwater, hustling to join his ticket as the vice presidential nominee. Goldwater, who considered Wallace a racist thug (and who also felt Wallace had little appeal outside the Deep South), didn't even dignify the overture with a response. But Goldwater was wrong, at least about the range of Wallace's appeal. Wallace's appeal *was* national, and it was an appeal precisely counter to Goldwater's own. Despite his radical platform, Goldwater was as grey as the suits he favoured – an anti-intellectual technocrat whose speech seethed without erupting. Wallace, who aspired to be as graceful as JFK, was a bit more like Hitler. Hunter S. Thompson, on the campaign trail as a journalist, described how awe-inspiring Wallace could be as an orator:

It was the first time I'd seen Wallace in person. There were no seats in the hall; everybody was standing. The air was electric even before he started talking, and by the time he was five or six minutes into his spiel I had a sense that the bastard had somehow levitated himself and was hovering over us. It reminded me of a Janis Joplin concert. Anybody who doubts the Wallace appeal should go out and catch his act sometime. He jerked this crowd around like he had them all on wires. They were laughing, shouting, whacking each other on the back ... it was a flat-out fire and brimstone *performance*.

Wallace said what Goldwater intimated. Where Goldwater advocated for 'state's rights' and voted against integration, Wallace said 'segregation now, segregation tomorrow, segregation forever', and stood in the doorway of the University of Alabama, in full view of the nation's press cameras, denying entrance to the first two black students invited to enrol. Wallace absolutely understood his audience. As his biographer, Dan T. Carter, argues: 'You can't explain Wallace's appeal to these people simply on the basis of their racism. Wallace, as a lifelong outsider, taps into working class and ethnic Americans' feelings of resentment, anger, frustration of being on the outside.'

Years later, his political life all but finished and his family fragmented, Wallace found God. Abandoning the persona of the racist agitator, he made peace with his enemies and asked for their forgiveness. His pleas struck a chord with black Alabamans, who, now able to vote, promptly helped elect him as governor for a final time. One of those old adversaries, black civil rights leader John Lewis, suggested that 'in a very strange sense he was somewhat reverting back to the old Wallace. Maybe, just maybe, to his true self'.

3.2 *George Wallace at the University of Alabama*

THE MAN WHO DIDN'T KNOW HIMSELF

In 1960, Richard Nixon won a third of black American votes and still lost the election to John F. Kennedy. Coming off the back of his vice presidency in the Eisenhower administration, Nixon was an incumbent of sorts. JFK, a Catholic, was the more unlikely candidate. He was also more likeable. There was simply no way that Nixon, an awkward man who didn't really like people, could compete with such charisma. When he ran again in 1968, mindful of his inadequacies and wary of the press he had so viciously lashed out at in 1962, his campaign was well prepared strategically and as a media organisation. He didn't, however, count on George Wallace as an opponent.

Bolstered by his reception with the public beyond the Deep South in 1964 but realistic about his chances of winning the Democratic nomination amidst a pool of strong, anti-war and pro-Civil Rights candidates, Wallace ran as a third-party independent for president in 1968. Thumbing his nose, he kicked off his campaign in Nixon's Southern California backyard, Orange County, because it was, in his view, 'full of nuts and kooks'. Wallace knew his audience, and Nixon watched in horror as his doppelgänger constructed a national platform around the same theme of 'restoring law and order', gathering steam with his ungodly performances. Surely this wouldn't be a repeat of 1960?

Nixon's fortitude was his not-so-secret weapon. Though he was never an all-American boy (Roger Ailes once quipped that Nixon 'was forty-two years old the day he was born'), he was recognisably a product of his culture and age – hard working, an unpolished striver more than a dreamy dreamer, tough and smart and dirty when he had to be. He was a middle child whose oldest and youngest siblings died in childhood, and was raised in the far-reaches of Los Angeles' exhausting sprawl by an abusive father and a doting mother who bequeathed him his life's most fateful lesson: that lying was bad, but really only if you got caught. Nixon had the tenacity and the backstory to win.

Nixon pivoted, running as a centrist between Wallace on the right and Hubert Humphrey, the Democratic nominee, to his left. Uncertain of *how* to craft a winning persona, never mind whether he could actually convincingly role-play it, Nixon also heavily relied on his real secret weapons – his 'opposition research' and communications teams – to guide his campaign strategy.

More specifically, Nixon's secret weapons when it came to strategy were Kevin Phillips, a pale and dour man his PR team called an 'ethnic specialist' and his fellow strategists dubbed 'The Computer', and John Maddox, a tall, thin, frowning man who was an expert in 'semantic differential marketing research'.

Phillips had put together maps of county-by-county US presidential election returns so he could track voting patterns; he would then delve into local histories to supplement his understanding of these patterns. His conclusion was something Wallace could have told him from instinct and experience: 'Politically, the US has not been a very effective melting pot. In practically every state and region, ethnic and cultural animosities and divisions exceed all other factors in explaining party choice and identification'.

Maddox had travelled around the United States asking people to describe the qualities that an ideal president would have, and to evaluate all three presidential candidates against that ideal. Plotting these data on a graph, he identified the personality traits that Nixon needed to improve if he wanted to win. 'Warmth' was the main problem area.

Prosaic in isolation, when these insights were brought together they were used to pioneer revelatory new message-targeting techniques.

For example, one Maddox report said 'the simple folksy manner of John Wayne can be effective with the target group'. With his knowledge of cultural geographies, Phillips could use such a nugget to help the communications team craft TV ads that would only play in carefully delineated regions of the country. So far, so market-leading. The challenge came in prepping Nixon for his live appearances.

Nixon came to television like he did to most things – grumpy and aloof, with what one journalist called 'an advertising man's approach to his work, acting as if he believed policies were products to be sold to the public – this one today, that one tomorrow, depending on the discounts and the state of the market'. Nixon, for his part, didn't see it like that, arguing in his hangdog way, 'people are much less impressed with image than columnists, commentators and pollsters. The American people may not like my face but they're going to listen to what I have to say'. In reality, they were deeply influenced by the images that Nixon's team crafted.

On TV, Nixon was successfully cast as the sensible, heartland candidate in the middle of a loony race, between an out-of-touch East Coast liberal (Hubert Humphrey) and an aggressive Southern nutcase (George Wallace). He was, in a sense, everything and nothing. In one ad, Nixon appealed to stoic, heroic Middle America – the industrious members of every race, ranging from corporate executives to blue-collar steelworkers. In Wallace country, he played on white voters' racial sentiments with an ad featuring a white woman walking achingly slowly down a dark street while a narrator describes how violent crime occurs in the US every 60 seconds (she's never attacked, but the suspense is masterful). In memos, his team brainstormed hard to come up with 'material that will make points with the Negro. These people are not particularly hostile to RN; they are indifferent to RN, and maybe some of them can be sold on RN'.

In the end, it wasn't necessary. In 1968, Nixon forfeited the black vote to Humphrey and the Deep South to Wallace and still won comfortably. In 1972, he effected the first great white switch, winning the Deep South from the Democrats (Wallace attempted to run, but was nearly killed by a

would-be assassin while campaigning in Maryland and had to drop out).
A year later, Kevin Phillips wrote an article headlined 'Conservative Chic',
predicting that Nixon would cement a coalition built around a managerial
class that 'merchandises the values that Middle Americans hold dear', using
the same combination of conservative economic policies and moderate
racial rhetoric. He was right about the coalition, but wrong about the candidate.

The Watergate scandal that ended his presidency was a by-product of
Nixon's belief that he was a fraud. The size of his 1972 victory (he won
every state except Massachusetts) felt like a great weight, and in victory
he sounded as bitter and petulant as he had in defeat. He'd won the entire
country, played it like a game of chess, but no one, he felt, was on his side.
Once an outsider, always an outsider. Who was he, really? In his memoirs,
Henry Kissinger, Nixon's secretary of state, wrote elegiacally of his former
boss:

> Nixon had set himself a goal beyond human capacity: to make himself
> over entirely; to create a new personality as if alone among all of man-
> kind he could overcome his destiny. But the gods exacted a fearful
> price for this presumption.

Weary from Watergate, the gods must have forgotten to exact the same
price from the master of reinvention, Ronald Reagan.

MASTERING THE ACT

Campaigning in 2008, Barack Obama succinctly summarised why Ronald Reagan's legacy casts such a long shadow:

> Reagan changed the trajectory of America in a way that Richard
> Nixon did not and in a way Bill Clinton did not. He put us on a fun-
> damentally different path because the country was ready for it. I think
> he tapped into what people were already feeling.

To the many Americans whose desperate nostalgia drew them to the insular idyll of suburbia, Ronald Reagan *personified* that golden American Arcadia. His biographer, Garry Wills, argued pithily that Reagan was 'the ideal past, the successful past, the hopeful future all in one'.

In short, to become president, Reagan perfectly applied all of the commandments I've presented so far:

1. He used his gut instincts and data insights to segment his audiences, from the core conservatives who'd championed him from his days as governor of California, to the Sunbelt Democrats he won over to the conservative cause in the 1980s.
2. He understood how the tumult of the sixties and seventies challenged his voters' hopes and exacerbated their fears, to the extent that these changing times seemed almost un-American – immoral, dogged by bureaucracy and devoid of opportunity.
3. He expertly crafted a persona that could authentically present a platform of hope, aspiration and the virtue of self-determination with thrillingly wide appeal – to conservatives of all stripes (libertarian, anti-communist and traditionalist), to swing voters and, indeed, to disillusioned liberals.

Reagan was so expert at cultivating his own myth that no single verifiable account of his childhood exists. As we know it, it reads a bit like Nixon's. Raised 100 miles west of Chicago in Dixon, Illinois by a dynamic mother and an alcoholic father, as a boy Reagan was happily poor but lonely for a bigger and better life. As an actor, he was frequently typecast as the character of young blade maturing to stout-hearted manhood, a hero's journey that anticipated his real-life transformation from impressionable liberal to pragmatic conservative. Reagan's politics began to change in Hollywood, when television disrupted the studio system, making stars more independent and entrepreneurial – and more interested in how much tax they were paying. The change was cemented when, newly divorced and his star on the wane, he began working with Lemuel Boulware at General Electric.

Boulware has been called the most influential American that most people have never heard of. As Vice President of Public and Community Relations, he created *GE Theater*, a primetime TV programme that was a blend of what today we'd call content marketing and good old-fashioned propaganda. Reagan, genial and easy to work with, was picked to host the show, which featured adverts for GE products, documentaries about how GE's industrial practices were shaping modern America, and light entertainment with a moral message. Boulware's goal was to bring GE's workers round to management's way of seeing things – that government regulation, union power and high taxation penalised risk-taking and inhibited innovation. His team, a kind of HR department staffed with social scientists, conducted market research amongst GE's workers, and with their insights, Boulware came to understand the working-class American mind better than any other executive. In Reagan he met his corporate soul mate; like George Wallace, Reagan understood working-class resentments and aspirations in his bones. Together, they used *GE Theater* to prime millions of Americans with libertarian conservative ideas. Equally importantly, as GE's pre-eminent spokesman-entertainer, the show gave Reagan the chance to dress rehearse the persona that would win him the role for which he now believed he was destined.

Reagan knew his audience, but they too were drawn to him. As a politician, his policies were heavily libertarian and anti-communist, but it was his authentic belief in traditional values that broadened his appeal to Americans who were waking up to the idea that they were, to one degree or another, socially conservative. So far, so Wallace. But unlike Wallace, Reagan projected a more positive view of the country's future, and nowhere was that more palatable to the mainstream than on the issue of race. As Wallace's biographer noted: 'Reagan showed that he could use coded language with the best of them, but even when he lashed out he always sounded like an avuncular uncle reluctantly scolding because he saw no alternative.' Reagan would simply say that his background made him 'incapable of prejudice', and that he thought any racial antagonism that lingered following Civil Rights could be dissolved culturally rather than via federal initiatives like affirmative action. That is, white Americans, being fair-minded and generous people, would welcome black Americans into their communities and workplaces until the playing field had truly levelled. By the end of his presidency, by a ratio of 3:1, black Americans thought that Reagan was racist. White Americans overwhelmingly reported that they identified with him and trusted him, even if they disagreed with his policy positions.

Reflecting on the difference in experience he had in coaching Nixon and Reagan, Roger Ailes marvelled at how audiences respond so unambiguously to speakers: 'I call it the magic bullet, because if your audience likes you they'll forgive just about everything else you do wrong. If they don't like you, you can hit every rule right on target and it doesn't matter.' Getting this right was Reagan's genius. He had been touted as presidential material ever since his televised 'A Time for Choosing' speech in 1964 on behalf of Barry Goldwater's doomed campaign. Anticipating a challenge in 1968, Nixon's speechwriter Ray Price wrote to his boss: 'Reagan's strength derives from personal charisma, glamour, but primarily the ideological fervour of the Right and the emotional distress of those who fear or resent the Negro, and who expect Reagan somehow to keep him "in his place".' Four years later, in the Oval Office tapes released to the public as part of the Watergate inquiry, Nixon was overheard dismissing Reagan as 'pretty shallow and of limited mental capacity'. Perhaps he was. But Reagan, ultimately, became *Ronald Reagan* by heeding the fatalistic advice that the Soviet premiere Nikita Khrushchev supposedly gave to Nixon:

'If the people believe there's an imaginary river out there, you don't tell them there's no river there. You build an imaginary bridge over the imaginary river.'

Nixon lied and paid the price. Reagan imagined, and the people believed.

3.3 *Reagan and Nixon face off*

What can we learn from Case story 3?

A crucial difference between a politician seeking election and an executive leading a change programme is usually the number of 'undecideds' who are up for grabs. For politicians, undecideds – swing voters – are a greater minority than opposition supporters who are highly unlikely to ever vote for you. For an executive, undecideds – employees who don't really know you, so have no particular reason to like you or loathe you – are often the majority. This circumstance favours the executive, who has a much larger pool of people to win over who are not predisposed against them. If you're that executive, and assuming you've done your homework by heeding the commandments given in Case stories 1 and 2, you're now ready to design a change persona that will appeal to the people you need to join your 'group' (i.e. be onside in the change programme).

Remembering that authenticity is a foundation you absolutely must build from, your persona can't be something you're not. It should be an amplification of your best self and so, like with all positive change, you've got to start by analysing yourself.

Psychologist Dan P. McAdams suggests there are three levels of personality:

1. Dispositional traits: essentially, what a person is like in general, in circumstances you and they would consider normal. Whenever you take a psychometric test you're testing your dispositional traits.
2. Characteristic adaptations: essentially, how people' personalities change when they're in abnormal situations, such as under pressure or intently focused on achieving something. The key word here is

'adaptations' – we behave differently in different abnormal situations, sometimes in ways that seem contradictory to our general personality traits. To make sense of a person's characteristic adaptations we need to understand their motivations and needs, their personal values and life goals.

3. Life narratives: essentially, how a person self-identifies and gives their own life meaning and purpose. Life narratives are internal to our selves – simplified and selective reconstructions of our pasts that are often connected to our hopes for the future.

The first step in designing your change persona is to understand your own personality. Dig out the results from those psychometric tests you've taken over the years – the ones you read once then chucked in a drawer – and write down the dispositional traits that stand out to you. If you've taken multiple tests, the traits you focus on may be the ones that are commonly reported from each of the tests; alternatively, they may just be the ones that feel most recognisably 'you' (and if you've never taken a psychometric test before, take a few online).

Next, make a list of your characteristic adaptations. First, identify a series of experiences of abnormal situations where someone commented on your behaviour, or where you consciously reflected on your own behaviour. What did they say – or what did you say to yourself? For example, an HR manager once told me that I had a reputation for being 'greedy' when it came to asking for salary increases. It's never nice to be accused of being greedy, and I wondered whether it was simply a negotiating tactic on her behalf. But even as I reflect on it today, I kind of know what she meant and where it comes from. In grey-area situations where there's no defined way forwards and in which I could lose out, I become totally single-minded and lose some of my self-awareness (and sometimes, unfortunately, my decorum). If ever I'm waiting in a queue where there's no defined line of people, I feel uneasy and I'll consciously make a mental note of everyone who was there before me and everyone who arrives after me. I'll demonstrably indicate to those I know were there before me that they should *go* before me, and if anyone who arrived after me tries to go before me – whether deliberately or because they're unsure of the etiquette – I'll make sure they don't get ahead of me. I've had more than my fair share of confrontations in airports as a result of this characteristic adaptation.

After considering the experiences that point to your own characteristic adaptations, you need to interpret what they suggest about your motivations, needs, values and goals. I don't think it's possible to trace a straight line from just one of my characteristic adaptations, like the one above, to my motivations etc., but given what I also know of my dispositional traits and my other characteristic adaptations, I think that it reflects the value that I place on order and merit (first come, first served), my need not to be seen to lose out in situations where I should 'win', and my motivations to always maximise my material reward (even at the risk of offending others, which I ruefully recognise is often short-sighted). None of this is easy, so it may also be helpful to ask those nearest and dearest to you to help you identify the scenarios and interpret them.

Finally, think of those life stories you often tell yourself or others, as a way of explaining how you see the world. Write them down and, again, look for commonalities to help you write a narrative statement that summarises your purpose in life. This is heavy, I know. For myself, leaping off from the scenario above, I think some of the following are important:

- When I was a kid, my dad told me that I should never hit people first, but if they hit me I should always hit back.
- I spent a significant part of my childhood in a British army community, where the size of the house you're given and the status of your family is closely linked to rank.
- As a teenager, I played in bands in my local punk-music scene, which taught me that creativity gets you noticed and that that kind of attention is an enjoyable form of power.

All these snippets of biography, I think, play into my overall internal life narrative, which goes something like this: I'm the product of modest stock, whose parents recognised that they had to search out opportunity overseas if they wanted a better life, given their existing means. It was a risk worth taking, but the rules of rank and hierarchy, while comforting in some ways, turned out to be extremely restrictive in others. As such, I hope to make a good, comfortable living for my family in self-employment, using my creativity and accumulated learning to work on projects I enjoy.

Once you feel you've got a handle on your personality, you can turn to designing your change persona.

A good place to start is with Jungian Archetypes. Carl Jung was a founding father of psychology, whose research led him to the conclusion that twelve universally understood character-types exist in the collective conscious of all humans, regardless of the country or culture they're from, or their individual experiences. Is that true? Who knows – but I think his archetypes are useful for two reasons:

1. They're recognisable. For each archetype I can always think of a few people I know who are like that archetype.
2. They're everywhere. In products, entertainment and religion. Marketers use them when designing brands, fiction writers use them to create story characters, and they underpin horoscopes and earth signs and the like.

The twelve archetypes are:

1. The Innocent	7. The Lover
2. The Everyman/woman	8. The Creator
3. The Hero	9. The Jester
4. The Caregiver	10. The Sage
5. The Explorer	11. The Magician
6. The Rebel	12. The Ruler

You should be able to get a sense of each archetype just by looking at the names. However, it's worth reading a little more about each one, which you can do on any number of websites.

Once you have a grasp of what each archetype means, identify three or four that most resonate with you and that you think, given your analysis of your own personality, are reflective of you.

Now look back at your audience segments. Which of the archetypes that you've identified as being reflective of yourself could strongly appeal to them all? It may be helpful to think about that cool person in your organisation that everyone likes. Which archetypes do you have in common with them?

At this stage you'll hopefully have one or two personas that reflect the best aspects of your personality and have appeal to your audience. You can now start to craft a change persona that amplifies the best of your traits in a bold and striking way, with strong emotional appeal to your people. Your persona will influence your approach to communication and the actions you take as you implement the change programme – which we'll cover in the final two parts of the book.

The purpose of your persona is to show that you're the same – part of the same tribe – as the people you're hoping will help make your organisational change a success. Humans are groupish animals, and loyalty is both materially and cognitively rewarding. Research shows that partisanship might be quite literally addictive, which makes sense when you think about religion and fan-worship. If you get it right, your persona can give you remarkable momentum through the power of goodwill from your followers.

PART II
Communicating change

CASE STORY 4

Freedom

Commandment

Ground your change vision in heritage and history, and lead with a promise to take your people 'back to the future'.

In-your-face patriotism went off the charts in the US in the aftermath of the 9/11 attacks. Overnight, American flags sprouted defiantly from sedate suburban lawns and began flapping angrily from the backs of pickup trucks. As a foreign exchange student it was hard to know how to act. The etiquette guide the university gave us warned us not to mistake chatty American friendliness for actual offers of friendship (i.e. don't be clingy). On campus, I was verbally attacked for naively wearing a Ho Chi Minh City t-shirt my parents had brought back from a trip to Vietnam. Americans didn't seem all that chatty or friendly, even superficially.

The stunned hurt and anger channelled gradually into a War on Terror patriot chic. There were even more flags everywhere by the summer of 2002, when three friends and I began an epic 7,000-mile road trip around the country. The Iraqis who ran the car rental place we used had a giant 'FBI Ten Most Wanted Fugitives' poster on the wall behind the counter with the same face in each of the top spots: Osama Bin Laden. There was still the feeling that an insurrectionary force might strike again, but the determination to let freedom reign manifested most visibly in support of the commercial market: America was standing strong, proudly open for business.

At least, most of it was. The 1990s brought seismic shifts in the dynamics of international trade and labour markets as the fall of the Berlin Wall brought down the entire Iron Curtain and China's long march in from the cold gathered pace. To stay competitive, American manufacturers increasingly moved their operations to the Sunbelt where they could take advantage of lower-cost, non-unionised labour (if they didn't just skip straight into Mexico or South-East Asia). The knock-on effects of these changes were starkly visible as we drove through deindustrialising 'Rustbelt' cities in Ohio, Indiana, Illinois and Iowa – weeds growing through cracks in the asphalt of main streets lined with boarded-up shops because the populations had declined so significantly in the absence of jobs.

In addition to the ubiquitous stars and stripes, there we began to notice the angry car bumper stickers:

The UN is NOT your friend!
Our Right To Bear Arms Does Not Make Us Villains.

4.1 *Angry bumper stickers, Iowa*

They added to the sense of depredation. On the car stereo we listened to big heartland rock anthems that celebrate the productivity of America's union-ised blue-collar classes; across the political spectrum from the progressive lament of John Mellencamp's 'Pink Houses' to Toby Keith's military tribute, 'Courtesy of the Red, White and Blue (The Angry American)'. West beyond the Indian reservations of South Dakota we wound up the Black Hills to Mount Rushmore. It was a mid-summer late afternoon, warm even as the sun was going down. On the plaza beneath the four famous faces, a family held hands in a circle and softly sang a hymn to America, a paean to its freedoms and prosperity. It was the kind of thing you see in a hokey movie. But years later I can remember it vividly and maturity helps me appreciate it more. It was genuine and modest, graceful in its thankfulness. Like the flags and bumper stickers and rock songs, but more so, it was evidence of the lasting power of the American Narrative – which, in the words of soci-ologist Christian Smith, goes like this:

> Once upon a time, our ancestors lived in an Old World where they were persecuted for religious beliefs and oppressed by established aristocracies. Land was scarce, freedoms denied, and futures bleak. But then brave and visionary men like Columbus opened a New World, and our freedom-loving forefathers crossed the ocean to carve out of a wilderness a new civilisation. Through bravery, inge-nuity, determination, and goodwill, our forebears forged a way of life where men govern themselves, believers worship in freedom, and where anyone can grow rich and become president. This America is genuinely new, a clean break from the past, a historic experiment in freedom and democracy standing as a city on a hill shining a beacon of hope to guide a dark world into a future of prosperity and liberty. It deserves our honour, our devotion, and possibly the commitment of our very lives for its defence.

It's not by accident that 'freedom' appears more frequently than any other word in this story. Freedom, as we'll see in Case story 5, is one of the foun-dations of human emotion, and that's partly why the American Narrative is so powerful. Yet Americans aren't unique in having emotionally compelling narratives to live by. All humans do, it's just that most of these other narratives haven't been as expertly mythologised and creatively communicated. In the US, the fire of the past is endlessly stoked to fuel that restless, unceasing ambition to seize the future. It was best expressed by F. Scott Fitzgerald in the last line of *The Great Gatsby*, a sentence so immortal it's undoubtedly a contender for the most-used quote in undergraduate essays: 'So we beat on, boats against the current, borne back ceaselessly into the past.' Politically, it's conservatives who have made most effective use of the national narrative.

So, the commandment for this case story is: Ground your change vision in heritage and history, and lead with a promise to take your people 'back to the future'.

TOBACCO AND THE TEA PARTY

With the scientific proof that cigarette smoke causes deadly diseases, the war against tobacco in the United States gathered force. It was fought in two arenas – the court of public opinion, via anti-smoking PR campaigns funded by non-profit groups such as the American Cancer Society and the American Lung Foundation, and in the courts of law, via state-government-sponsored litigation. In both arenas, Big Tobacco fought hard. But by the late 1970s, the industry was in a quandary: how could companies possibly grow when the future of their astonishingly lucrative staple product was under threat?

Most American tobacco companies began to diversify into food and drink. Philip Morris acquired Kraft Foods and Nabisco to become the largest food producer in the US, while behind the scenes a cold war was being fought for the soul of the company. There were two factions. The science-minded 'Hercules' side believed that Philip Morris should only continue making cigarettes until they had successfully established themselves as a food conglomerate. The sales-focused 'Atlas' group believed the company would always have to shoulder the burden of slinging tobacco. For a time, Hercules was the expected victor. However, by the early 1980s, the Office of the US Trade Representative helped open new markets for American tobacco in heavy-smoking Asian countries such as Japan, South Korea and Thailand; a decade later, Philip Morris was paying Margaret Thatcher £500,000 a year to help crack the former Soviet republics of central Europe, and China. By the time the hawk-nosed Australian Geoffrey Bible became CEO in 1994, the Atlas faction had triumphed: Philip Morris would, once again, focus purely on tobacco. It was just too much of a guaranteed money-spinner.

Still, a challenge remained. By the time Bible's Atlas strategy was affirmed, Philip Morris' public image was dirt amongst Americans. As Christopher Buckley's best-selling novel, *Thank You for Smoking*, lampooned, everyone knew smoking was deadly, but still the tobacco industry maintained the charade, using clean-cut, good-looking spokesmen to insist (with a winning smile) that no one could say for sure that cigarettes kill. To survive in the long term, the company needed a new narrative and it was gifted this by its opposition: if there was anything that the public disliked more than capitalists selling death it was sanctimonious 'neo-puritans' waging a war against an individual's right to do whatever the hell they wanted with their life, health-be-damned. As far as most Americans were concerned, it was still a free country, right?

The ammunition needed to develop the new narrative was substantial. For starters, freedom-hating tyrants such as Hitler and Napoleon had also hated smoking. So too had the Old World aristocrats Louis XIV and James I. Tobacco was patriotic: America's founding fathers had grown it and tobacco leaves are carved into the columns of the Capitol Building in Washington DC. Volumes of supportive letters sent to tobacco companies endorsed the idea that smoking was a sign of a free society, as one customer's letter maintained:

> I don't believe the lung association can prove anything. With so many other things in the air, where you work etc! I love to smoke – why don't people mind their own business … this country is getting just like Russia. No rights!

Former smoker Stephen King published a short story, 'The Ten O Clock People', about put-upon smokers who, by virtue of the habit about which they're made to feel unceasingly guilty, can see that alien creatures are attempting to take over humanity and that only they can defeat them. The zeitgeist pointed true north: in a free society, freedom of choice means freedom to smoke.

4.2 *Tobacco leaves on the Capitol Building, Washington DC*

The first mention of the Boston Tea Party as a historical locus for the new freedom narrative was in a free smokers' rights rag, *Philip Morris Magazine*, in 1989, in an article titled 'A Tea Party – Boston Style':

> The most famous protest in American history took place on the chilly night of December 16, 1773. Under cover of darkness, a group of American colonists boarded three British merchant ships … The men taking part in this protest of taxation without representation

were prominent businessmen and political leaders … They roused the three British captains from their beds and told them why they had come. They assured them that neither their crews nor their ships would be hurt if they didn't try to resist or interfere with the business of the evening … Hundreds stood and watched from shore. But no one spoke. No orders were shouted. There were no cheers. The only sounds were the grunts of men, the splintering of wood, and the splash of heavy objects being dropped over the side, as dozens of chests of heavily taxed British tea were tossed overboard.

Further down, it spelled out the point:

British policies of minority rule, increased government intervention, unfair taxation – ironically, those same issues face us again today. Excise taxes, advertising restrictions, franchise legislation and smoking bans make it necessary to act to our protect our rights as citizens of the United States.

It's likely the Tea Party reference was influenced by the 'tea bag rebellion' of 1988, when conservative talk radio hosts encouraged people to send tea bags through the mail to Capitol Hill in protest against a motion to increase congressional wages by 51% (people responded in droves and the wage hike was defeated). But it was an apt choice for Philip Morris – after all, Paul Revere, the patriot who rode through the towns of New England to alert American militias of the coming of the British at the beginning of the War of Independence, was essentially a prototype for the Marlboro Man.

Nevertheless, it took an outside PR agency to recognise the universal power of the theme. In 1992, Gary Auxier, an Executive Vice President at Burson-Marsteller, wrote an impassioned proposal outlining his idea: what if a new American tax revolution could be organised under the banner of a modern-day Tea Party, that combined the momentum of grassroots movements and the financial muscle of corporate elites to promote a political narrative that could not be ignored?

BACK TO THE FUTURE

Auxier's proposal was written for the Coalition Against Regressive Taxation (CART), a lobbying group organised by Big Tobacco to build support across industries with an interest in rolling back excise taxes. It was novel in two ways:

1. Unlike most corporate lobbying efforts, it proposed that CART be aggressively clear about its anti-tax position. So as not to appear too self-serving, it should leverage the public's anti-big-government mood to demonstrate support for its position.
2. It would aim to create a media phenomenon around this grassroots 'movement', recruiting a diversity of activist groups to its cause, including those representing women's and minority rights and others that campaigned for local business rights.

Early attempts to make the concept work failed. But they struck a chord with Rich Fink, co-founder of Citizens for a Sound Economy, a group that contributed funds to CART. To Fink, the concept was bigger than a corporate effort to defeat an excise tax increase; it was nothing less than the foundation of the American Narrative. It was not, as many CART members envisioned, simply about stopping legislation in its tracks but about correcting the historical course. The 'New Boston Tea Party' was a vehicle for going back to the future: for reclaiming the American Narrative and using it to construct a political infrastructure that could lead to that promised American Arcadia. In the language of the 21st century, the Tea Party was a brand.

Its big moment came in 2009 when Barack Obama announced his healthcare reform bill. As Auxier had originally intended, it brought together a variety of groups: the 'astroturf' (fake grassroots) lobbying group The Tea Party Express and the genuine grassroots coalition of Tea Party Patriots; the attention-getting accoutrements of 'Don't Tread on Me' snake flags and the three-cornered American Revolution hats; the emotive language of the 'tyranny' of Obama's 'socialism'. Tea Party events became brand experiences that the media helped to amplify, most prominently with Glenn Beck on Fox News, who would work himself into a crying fit to heighten the emotion as he championed Tea Partiers as courageous underdogs fighting to correct that future course. But the reason the anti-ObamaCare Tea Party worked so well was not immediately visible.

4.3 *Tea Party protesters, St. Cloud, Minnesota*

Fink and the political strategists who coordinated the Tea Party movement of 2009 laid the sub-narratives of American Exceptionalism, biblical fundamentalism and free market prosperity atop one another and emphasised that they are one and the same. Each has a touchstone text – respectively, the American Constitution, the Old Testament and Adam Smith's *The Wealth of Nations* – that posits brave risk-taking as the surest path to individual freedom, and each of these texts' lessons, its followers believe, has been subverted by the growth in size and reach of the federal government. Tea Party speakers would incorporate religious language into their fiscal conservative rhetoric, calling the Tea Party the 'Great Awakening' and pointing out that the federal government flouts the commandment 'thou shalt not steal' because it attempts to redistribute income by legislating 'stealing bills'. At rallies, speakers would first talk about emotional subjects like how socialism would rob individuals of their rights and freedoms, fluffing their audiences into a frenzy of indignation before libertarian economists took the stage to outline the arcana of policies for which Tea Partiers should vote.

It worked. Although research showed that, when explained in lay terms, most Americans disagreed with Tea Party policies, nearly a third of the elec-torate ended up voting for Tea Party politicians in the 2010 Congressional elections (overwhelmingly across the Sunbelt and parts of the Rustbelt).

The lasting legacy of the Tea Party may well be the aspect of it that was most mocked by liberal journalists like Thomas Frank:

> Management-speak saturates the movement. Tea Partiers sometimes write about 'core competence' when they mean *protesting*, 'political entrepreneurs' when they mean *leaders*, and 'early adopters' when they mean *rank and file*. There even used to be a Tea Party website that kept a list of favourite CEOs.

Amidst the jumble of ideas and ideologies that resonated with the Tea Party was the theme of producerism. Later, a Harvard study showed that Tea Partiers didn't much care whether federal welfare programmes reflected free market economic theory. What they did focus on was whether the people on welfare deserved to receive it. It made sense: in the aftermath of the 2008 financial crisis, unemployment or underemployment affected up to 30% of the American labour force and seemingly safe investments such as property and retirement accounts had been decimated. Tea Party ire, borne of the frustration, desperation and wounded pride of homeowners, taxpayers and school parents was, once again, directed at 'freeloaders' and bureaucrats. Their respect and admiration was reserved for entrepreneurs who had achieved the dream of independent wealth and created jobs in the process.

It's this that led American conservatism to Donald Trump.

What can we learn from Case story 4?

It's worth reminding ourselves of some of the insights from Case story 1 at this stage. People are contrary but they're also quite predictable:

1. People are neophilic and neophobic. They want new things but are afraid of things that are too unfamiliar.
2. People are groupish and individualistic. They want to be accepted as members of particular social groups, yet be unique and different to others.
3. People want to be sheep and wolves. They want to be known for their traditional manners and classic tastes, as well as for being unpredictable and cutting edge.

In summary, we have a reverence for the past and a yearning for the future. The creators of successful brands, ideas and cultural identities understand this, and their creations reconcile an outlook on the past with a concept of the future in ways that have strong meaning to particular groups of people. To successfully reconcile a perspective on the past with a vision of the future you've got to develop a believable and emotionally persuasive argument along the lines of 'this is how we are as a type of people, which is why we should do a specific thing if we want to be happy'. This is a narrative.

Your change vision should be a narrative that connects the past – heritage and history – to a future promise and purpose that your people will fulfil. The *context* for this is the culture of your organisation (as identified using the lessons from Case story 1), but fundamentally this change vision is NOT about your organisation: it's about your *people* (again, as segmented using lessons from Case story 1). It's not about new markets, innovation and meeting the challenges posed by competitors or regulators, it's about destiny, promise and outwitting antagonists. I call this a 'back to the future' narrative.

Pragmatic leaders sometimes push back against this kind of thing, arguing that 'soft and fuzzy' stuff rubs smart and savvy people the wrong way and could make them feel cynical and detached. In fact, the opposite is true. Research shows that people do not reason in search of truth so much as they reason in support of their emotional reactions to things. In other words, we look for a moral reason to justify our emotional or instinctive responses to things and apply a conscious rationale retrospectively. Indeed, good reasoning *requires* emotional power: people whose brains have been damaged in areas that remove their emotionality make poor rational decisions. As such, a 'back to the future' narrative that's well calibrated to your people, referencing experiences that they've lived and using language and phrases that activate powerful mental associations, will be irresistible. A good 'back to the future' narrative reinforces for people what they think they are, and justifies their positive emotional response to it. Conversely, and perhaps counter-intuitively, an overly rational narrative that relies on numerical data and pure logic is likely to be perceived as earnest and naïve, simply because no one likes to be blinded with science.

To get started with developing your 'back to the future' narrative, you need to define:

1. the narrative motivator
2. a narrative title
3. the narrative structure
4. the narrative stages.

Your narrative motivator is often called the 'why' – the reason change and an associated narrative is needed. The motivator threads throughout the narrative and provides its momentum or thrust. Some examples of 'back to the future' narrative motivators for organisations are:

- an outside threat to our way of life means we need to build protections around the things that made us prosperous in the first place;
- the regulatory establishment is not managing a crisis well so we must take matters into our hands if we're to continue with our mission;
- ignoble competitors are corrupt and our revulsion for the way they behave means we must act quickly to check their progress and preserve our place in the world.

If change starts at the top, it also starts with a title. You can't write a vision and create a plan around it without a strong title. There's a reason CART built their campaign around 'The New Boston Tea Party': it was more vivid, resonant and provocative a title than simply 'Coalition Against Regressive Taxation'. As you brainstorm your change narrative motivator, focus also on writing a great title (even if it is only a working title that changes as the other pieces fall into place).

Once you have a narrative motivator and title, you can begin to plot the storyline, starting with narrative structure. Your narrative structure is essentially a beginning, middle and end, such as:

Beginning	Middle	End
1. The past	1. The present	1. The future
2. The world as it is today	2. A threat that arises	2. A way to defeat the threat
3. Problem	3. Solution	3. Impact of solution

I'd start with a generic structure using one of the suggestions above, and then make it your own by defining sub-headings. For example, the 'New Boston Tea Party' structure and sub-headings might have been the following:

Beginning	Middle	End
The world as it is today, or 'Freedom makes America great and strong'	A threat that arises, or 'Federal taxation threatens our freedoms'	A way to defeat the threat, or 'A coalition of the willing to preserve our freedoms'

You then need to fill in the copy underneath each sub-heading. Using tried-and-tested story elements will help with this:

- genesis
- introduce protagonists and antagonists
- change catalyst
- adventure (which can include obstacles in your path, challenges to overcome and a possible clash between protagonists and antagonists)
- the outcome of your adventure
- promise
- newfound purpose.

These are the story elements of the American Narrative:

Protagonists: brave, freedom-loving visionaries

Antagonists: oppressive, narrow-minded aristocrats

Genesis: persecution in the Old World, where scarcity and miserliness reigned

Change catalyst: Columbus discovering the New World

Adventure: crossing the ocean in search of freedom and carving out a civilisation from the wilderness

Outcome of adventure: forging a way of life where men govern themselves, believers worship in freedom, and where anyone can grow rich and become president

Promise: the equal right of all to live a free and abundant life regardless of social class

Newfound purpose: defending a democracy that serves as a beacon of hope to the rest of the world.

The story elements of the American Narrative fit into the structure as follows:

Beginning	Middle	End
- Genesis - Introduce protagonists and antagonists - Change catalyst	- Adventure	- Outcome of your adventures - Promise - Newfound purpose

Here it is in full:

Beginning	'*Once upon a time, our ancestors* [protagonists] *lived in an Old World where they were persecuted for religious beliefs* [genesis] *and oppressed by established aristocracies* [antagonists]. *Land was scarce, freedoms denied, and futures bleak* [genesis]. *But then brave and visionary men like Columbus opened a New World* …' [change catalyst]
Middle	'… *And our freedom-loving forefathers* [protagonists] *crossed the ocean to carve out of a wilderness a new civilisation through bravery, ingenuity, determination, and goodwill.*' [adventure]
End	'… *Our forebears forged a way of life where men govern themselves, believers worship in freedom, and where anyone can grow rich and become president* [outcome of adventure]. *This America is genuinely new, a clean break from the past, a historic experiment in freedom and democracy standing as a city on a hill shining a beacon of hope to guide a dark world into a future of prosperity and liberty* [promise]. *It deserves our honour, our devotion, and possibly the commitment of our very lives for its defence.*' [newfound purpose]

Finally, if you're lacking inspiration in trying to think outside the strictures of organisational life to come up with a change narrative for your people, consider that many sub-narratives of the American Narrative neatly map to recognisable concepts of professional life:

Sub-narrative of the American Narrative	Concept from professional life
The Constitution …	… Code of conduct
American Exceptionalism …	… Culture
Independent wealth …	… Measure of success
The frontier …	… Growth markets
The American Dream …	… Personal development goals

The way these things are written tends to make them quite dry and boring to read. Nevertheless, the concepts and policies that they enshrine are important to people because they provide structure, meaning and security. They could be valuable totems that you can reference in your 'back to the future' change vision.

Remember, somewhere in every organisation are the seeds of a drama that express its value to employees. The secret of effective change is not rational explanations that justify new company structures and processes, but understanding why that drama motivates people. Use that drama to craft a change vision that gets your people excited about change.

Entertainment

Commandment

Use the principles of entertainment to educate and engage people in service of your change vision.

If you've ever doubted the capacity of entertainment to change the world, it's worth remembering that a couple of comedians very nearly got Bill Clinton kicked out of office.

As the case for impeachment gathered pace with the revelation that the president had lied about sexual relations with Monica Lewinsky, Hillary Clinton appeared on prime-time breakfast TV and alleged: 'The great story here is this vast right-wing conspiracy that has been conspiring against my husband since the day he announced for president.' Betsey Wright, deputy chair of the 1992 Clinton presidential campaign, dismissed rumours of Clinton's frequent extramarital affairs as 'bimbo eruptions', a phrase that lit the spark for conservative talk-radio host Rush Limbaugh's unrelenting mockery of Bill's flagrant philandering. Limbaugh, essentially a stand-up comic who preferred the radio booth to a stage, regularly created skits and songs that skewered Clinton's behaviour, with impressionist Paul Shanklin mimicking the president's unmistakable southern twang. Across the centre of the political spectrum, the critical reaction to Hillary's charge was that she was being paranoid. After all, Bill *had* lied, and sending up political figures was a time-honoured comedy tradition. But Hillary was right to be worried.

The year the Clintons arrived in the White House, Ronald Reagan (or 'Ronaldus Maximus', as Rush refers to the hero he never met) wrote Limbaugh a letter awarding him the conservative crown: 'Now that I've retired from active politics, I don't mind that you have become the Number One voice for conservatism in our Country.' It was a deserved and prescient accolade. Limbaugh was on air eighteen hours a week with a nationally syndicated show. Since 1987 his radio show has consistently been the most popular commercial radio programme in the United States (in 2019 he maintained the top spot with 15.5 million listeners a week). Through the Clinton years Limbaugh maintained he was simply an entertainer, but Hillary recognised him as one of her own: a savvy politico and sophisticated propagandist whose influence helped conservative Republicans to frustrate the Clintons' change agenda.

The comedic attacks on Bill's infidelity marked a disturbing acceleration of partisan division. Reagan had already proved that the way to convert people to the conservative cause was with appeals to the heart, not the head. To argue that Clinton's behaviour, while reprehensible, did not necessarily impact on his ability to govern, was reasonable. So Limbaugh, proudly *unreasonable*, used satire like a knife to the heart to make the case that Clinton's transgressions were a mark of his liberalness. Stanky liberal behaviour just proved that liberalism – where its sympathies lay and what its policies aimed to do – was inherently corrupt and misguided. Limbaugh had discovered that partisan humour was a deadly weapon. By making people laugh viciously *with* him at the Clintons, Limbaugh was building rapport with the millions of Americans who listened in. With his trademark humiliation humour, Limbaugh laid the groundwork for the transformation of right-leaning news media into what David Frum calls 'the conservative entertainment industry'.

In so doing, Limbaugh and his fellow 'talkers' have created a new American conservative identity. Limbaugh's influence is noticeable everywhere today: in the bro culture of Vince Vaughan movies, contemporary country music, corporate America and professional sports. He's influenced Donald Trump's political persona and his policies – Trump regularly listens in and takes cues about how to frame and position policy from the man who writes the lingua franca of 21st-century American conservatism.

So, the commandment for this case story is: Use the principles of entertainment to educate and engage people in service of your change vision.

5.1 *Golf buddies: Rush Limbaugh and Donald Trump*

ARGUMENT IS ENTERTAINING

Ironically, the man who started it all was a scion of the North-Eastern Republican elite so despised by conservatives. In most outward respects, William F. Buckley Jr was stereotypical of his class: born into privilege, he was privately schooled in France and England, went to university in Mexico, served as a teenage officer in the US Army during World War II, enrolled at Yale and, upon graduation, was recruited to the CIA. But in one important respect, his background was different. Unlike the majority of his well-heeled peers, Buckley was not a WASP (white Anglo-Saxon protestant). Buckley's family were devout Catholics, and much like the Kennedys – that other Catholic American dynasty – they formed a fringe of the establishment. As a young man, Buckley embraced early-20th-century libertarianism and the small 'c' conservatism of social tradition, order and hierarchy. But Catholicism gave Buckley what would forever, for him, be the defining trait of American conservatism: rebellion against the status quo. To his brother, Reid Buckley, 'Bill was a conservative right-wing libertarian Christian – but most of all Bill was a revolutionary'.

If Catholicism was his rudder, Yale was the crucible of Buckley's lasting legacy. At Yale, Buckley viscerally came up against a truism of mid-century American society: liberal thought dominated the nation's organs of power and influence. Liberalism was so endemic that the New York intellectual Lionel Trilling actually *complained* in 1950 that 'liberalism is not only the dominant but even the sole intellectual tradition'. Buckley, well-bred with the airs, graces and confidence of the worldly-wise, bristled with resentment when professors dismissed his ideas and outlook. These experiences crystallised his argument in *God and Man at Yale*, the book that would make him famous: that America was divided into two groups of people – the 'university crowd' and the 'non-university crowd' – and the small, compromised elite that made up the former was not only indoctrinating students, but, via its mass influence, suppressing the intrinsically conservative beliefs of the latter.

At Yale, Buckley also honed his entertainment weapon of choice: debate. In 1955, flush with the controversial success of *God and Man at Yale*, Buckley founded *National Review*. His aim was to create a magazine that could reach the Main Street bookstores of Middle America and expose people to ideas from across the three strands of nascent conservatism: libertarianism, traditionalism and anti-communism. Its purpose, in the words of publisher William A. Rusher, was brutally clear: '*National Review* would be militantly *engagé*, dedicated to waging political war against the liberals rather than merely restating conservative principles in some safely abstract form'. Its editors declared that they were at war with 'satanic' communism, prophesied the coming of a 'Third World War' and pilloried political, cultural and business leaders who dared disagree with them. The journal's circulation boomed with a readership that transcended political fault lines. Centrist academic Clinton Rossiter summed up its appeal when he wrote: '*National Review* continues to interest, amuse and anger me, and what more can I ask of a magazine?'

The success of *National Review* led to *Firing Line*, the TV debate show Buckley hosted from 1966 to 1999 and which gave him his biggest platform yet. The debonair Buckley could be arch and wry, coy and arrogant, all in the space of one verbose attack. In a sense, Buckley was never really that interested in the non-university crowd. He was intent on humiliating the intellectual left, who, Reid Buckley felt,

> were never hesitant about smearing anyone from the right wing. That was a battle that Bill had to fight all the time. If you are a right-winger you don't want to have anything to do with the gnostic heresies of Nazism and fascism. And that was a label that the left wing kept trying to pin on the right wing.

These kinds of accusations themselves made for intrigue and entertainment. But Bill's verbal counterpunch served as an emotionally intoxicating call-to-arms for non-university conservatives across America. This wolf in sheep's clothing sided with *them*.

With *National Review* and *Firing Line*, Buckley brought conservatism to the mainstream. He intimately understood the contradictory human need to belong and the desire to rebel against conformity. He recognised that argument was entertaining. Knowing this, he created a brand of political entertainment that rallied people from across America to the conservative cause.

5.2 *Bill Buckley*

PARODY AND POLEMIC

In 1988, on the eve of his move across the country from the capital of California, Sacramento, to the capital of American culture, New York City,

Rush Limbaugh wrote a column in the *Sacramento Union* titled '35 Undeniable Truths'. Quoting axioms by as diverse a pantheon of white men as Thomas Hobbes, Norman Mailer, John D. Rockefeller, Billy Graham, Paul McCartney and his own father, Limbaugh articulated his unapologetically un-PC worldview. Limbaugh used celebrity quotes because he had so little worldly experience. Of communism and war, abortion and religious belief, Limbaugh knew nothing. He arrived in New York an affluent hick from small-town Missouri who had, until his mid thirties, been so apolitical and detached that he had only first registered to vote a few years earlier. Still, he was a rising conservative star and, ever courteous, Bill Buckley invited Rush to attend a *National Review* editorial meeting.

Buckley was handing the conservative media baton to a brash upstart from across a gaping cultural chasm that bespoke just how drastically the sixties and seventies had forever changed America. Uncharacteristically nervous, Limbaugh waited in the foyer of Buckley's Park Avenue apartment amidst artefacts and trophies that told of his host's many interests – accomplished musician, world-class sailor, proficient skier, amateur boxer, spy-fiction novelist. In stark contrast, Limbaugh hated physical exertion and cultural pursuits, once claiming that he'd go to museums only when they got golf carts to ride around in. He was ushered into Buckley's inner sanctum as the editors were discussing whether James Joyce could have published *Ulysses* in the late 20th century; Limbaugh, intellectually lazy, had no idea what they were talking about. Nevertheless, Buckley readily befriended Limbaugh, a man he recognised as a wise fool whose moment had arrived.

In 1987, Ronaldus Maximus made one of his less famous but most consequential acts of deregulation when he repealed the Fairness Doctrine, a federal regulation that required TV and radio networks to be demonstrably fair and balanced in their broadcasts on controversial issues. Conservatives, who resented the principles of objectivity as a tool of left-leaning media to constrain freedom of speech, recognised earlier than most that this opened a Pandora's box of opportunity. Controversial issues no longer needed debate; instead, they could be fashioned into wedge issues to encourage listeners to take a specific stance themselves. Rather

than simply *informing* an amorphous mass of people, conservative media
folk could instead *cultivate* an audience with directly partisan appeal. In
the first six years after the repeal of the Fairness Doctrine, more than a
thousand radio stations switched to a talk-radio format, with conservative
on-air minutes outnumbering liberal minutes by a ratio of 10:1. It worked.
Listeners who liked a presenter's position on a divisive wedge issue would
not only continue to listen in, but would become more resolute on the
topic because someone on air – in a position of authority – held the same
opinion.

It held that the opposite was also true: listeners who disliked what they
were hearing would drop off. For Rush Limbaugh this wasn't the case. He
was the most successful beneficiary of the repeal of the Fairness Doctrine
in its immediate aftermath because his listenership covered the political
spectrum. Political journalist John Fund observed:

> The rap on conservatives always was they didn't have any sense of
> humour, they couldn't tell a joke, they were pessimistic and had a
> crabby view of the world. Well Rush is none of those things. He's very
> optimistic, he believes America's best days are ahead of us, much like
> Ronald Reagan did. He certainly can tell a joke – even a lot of liberals
> find him very funny. He's taken many of the conservative stereotypes
> and turned them on their head.

Limbaugh blew up conservative stereotypes using, in his words, a sig-
nature trick he learned from Mohammad Ali: 'illustrating the absurd by
being absurd'. Building on an instinct for practical jokes, Limbaugh coined
a stylised, satirical lingo to paint a cartoonish world where feminazis,
environmentalist wackos, commie pinkos suffering from battered liberal
syndrome and the state-run media do their best to defeat Chief Waga-Waga
El Rushbo and the racist, sexist, bigot, homophobes of the El Conservo
Tribe. It's an underdog's braggadocio that's irresistible to the downtrod-
den taxpayers, struggling homeowners and befuddled school parents who
are today the squeezed middle of post-Great Recession America. Hazel
Staloff, a long-time Limbaugh fan, explained his appeal as 'a kind of almost

narcotic effect on listeners that you think, no matter how horrible the world is, or how scared you are, that it can get better'.

By the time Bill Buckley accepted him as his heir apparent, Limbaugh had begun to take his role as an edutainer – part entertainer, part educator – seriously. By the 2000s he was referring to himself as a 'weapon of mass instruction' and holder of the 'prestigious Attila the Hun Chair at the Limbaugh Institute for Advanced Conservative Studies'. Slowly but surely, his shows devoted less time to parody and became more like lectures on wonkish policy issues such as healthcare reform and budgetary restraint. In a rare interview from 2008, Limbaugh admitted: 'I want to persuade people with ideas. I don't walk around thinking about my power. But in my heart and soul, I know I have become the intellectual engine of the conservative movement.'

***

Rush Limbaugh's soul brother in the conservative media elite was Roger Ailes, the TV producer and communications consultant who founded Fox News. Ailes was ten years older than Limbaugh, but in so many respects they were uncannily similar – fleshy, rotund small-town Midwesterners who were instinctually rather than ideologically conservative, a corn-fed Tweedledum and Tweedledee with a penchant for caustic profanity. Yet beneath the surface there were differences. Limbaugh found immediate success with parody, but began to move away from it as his influence grew. Ailes' early preferred style was cordiality, and he would only champion polemic in the post-9/11 years when Fox became the leading news channel in the United States. Limbaugh, encouraged to make the move to TV by Ailes, found quickly that it wasn't for him. Ailes, on the other hand, had a near-religious belief in the power of television.

This conviction gave him his start in broadcasting. As executive producer on a daytime talk show that broadcast from Ailes' home state of Ohio, he hosted Richard Nixon. 'It's a shame a man has to use gimmicks like this to get elected,' Nixon told him. 'Television', Ailes admonished, 'is not a gimmick'. Ailes struck Nixon as a man who knew how to use TV as a weapon and he hired him to the campaign team. It was a good decision. Where cultural critics and commentators of the time focused on the detached passivity of the TV-watching experience, Ailes argued otherwise, pointing to its near-magical power to transfix both performers and viewers:

> I once knew a TV sales manager who couldn't describe the miracle of television. So when people asked him what he did for a living he said 'I sell pictures that fly through the air'. That may be the best description I've ever heard. Because TV is a miracle we act the way we do in the presence of all miracles – we change our behaviour. Because there's something mysterious about it, it's intimidating. And consequently we often act unlike ourselves when a TV camera is present.

Asked to provide advice to Ronald Reagan in anticipation of a TV debate during the 1984 election campaign, Ailes told the befuddled president, 'You got elected on themes. Every time a question is asked, relate it to one of your themes. You know enough facts, and it's too late to learn new ones now anyway.' During the debate, in response to a question from reporter Henry Trewhitt about whether he was too old to be president, Reagan's riposte that he would not exploit his opponent's youth and inexperience was, for Ailes, the perfect example of how *a person is the message they wish to deliver*:

> When you communicate with someone, it's not just the words you choose to send to the other person that make up the message. You're also sending signals about what kind of person you are – by your eyes, your facial expression, your body movement, your vocal pitch, tone, volume, and intensity, your commitment to your message, your sense of humour and many other factors.

Across the dais, as Reagan took a sip of water, even his opponent, Walter Mondale, was grinning like a Cheshire cat. The old man was just too likeable.

Back then, likeability was the most elevated skill in Ailes' philosophy:

> If you take care of all four essentials well – be prepared, be comforta-
> ble and put others at ease, be committed, be interesting – you'll be an
> excellent communicator who never disappoints your audience. But
> if you can add likeability to these four essentials, you'll be a master
> communicator.

He cautioned cantankerous corporate and conservative heavyweights
that 'open displays of ill temper will almost insure unlikeability'. That all
changed with Fox News.

Ailes was left out in the cold by CNBC when it merged with Microsoft and
decided the right-leaning network he ran was too partisan. He had a point
to prove, and Rupert Murdoch didn't flinch when Ailes told him he needed
a billion dollars up front that he may never see again. Fox News hit the
airwaves of Middle America in 1996 with an indignant splash. In the midst
of the various scandals that dogged Bill Clinton during his time in office,
Fox News pioneered a form of reporting that closely followed the rules of
adrenalin-fuelled entertainment:

1. create suspense with dramatic music and graphics that cue up a provocative headline;
2. stir anger and excitement with news stories that use language with
   strong moral and associative meaning;
3. deliver emotional catharsis via an outraged polemic from a Fox presenter or commentator.

Each aspect is un-subtle in its appeal to self-identified conservatives:

- patriotic music and graphics that reference the American flag;
- language that's straight out of the conservative glossary, like 'limited
  government', 'balanced budgets', 'reckless spending' and 'constitu-
  tional principles';

- ill-tempered presenters and commentators, distasteful to casual observers, are seen as bold and authoritative no-bullshit types.

The historic impact of the Fox network on the news can't be overstated. 'Fox is the ultimate surrender of news to entertainment,' says journalism professor Mark Danner. 'Ailes pioneered the unembarrassed consequences of the recognition that news is entertainment. His influence has been so great that it is now hard to recognise it.'

5.3 *Roger Ailes caricature*

MIGHTY TROGLODYTI

The internet has reinforced the primacy of talk radio and TV broadcasting as the most popular formats in the conservative entertainment industry. Rush Limbaugh's listeners and Fox News viewers can access the same content online that they can catch in real time on the air. Nevertheless, the mobile-led social web has contributed significantly to the development of the conservative ecosystem over the past decade in much the same way that it's affected every other subculture: it's become more radical and fanatical. These changes influenced Limbaugh to focus more on policy than parody, and Fox News hosts to be more fervently polemical. According to a political quotient test created by three American academics, including Steve Levitt of Freakonomics fame, Fox became more conservative after 2009, coinciding with the election of Obama, the rise of the Tea Party, the mainstreaming of social media and the hiring of Glenn Beck.

Beck burst forth on Fox like a troglodyte child of Limbaugh and Ailes. Though his formative career was similar to Limbaugh's (he started out as an apolitical talk-radio prankster), his personal story was more tumultuous: his drug-addict mum drowned when he was thirteen, a possible suicide, and Beck inherited her struggles with alcohol, drugs and depression. That history informed his Fox News persona, described by Ailes' biographer Zev Chafets as 'nerdy professor, slapstick comic, born-again preacher, shock jock, weepy recovering addict, man of destiny – all [fighting] for airtime with chaotic results'. Arianna Huffington warned of the dangers of his 'paranoid style', and Thomas Frank coined the term 'orgasmaclysym' to describe the way Beck's talk of impending doom drove his viewers into a frenzy of fear and ecstasy.

Eventually fired by Fox, Beck also left the Republican Party and reinvented himself as an Independent conservative media mogul. He founded The Blaze TV, which he modelled on the *Huffington Post* as an alternative source of news to the mainstream media. Today, there's a plethora of online conservative provocateurs affiliated with The Blaze whose genders, ethnicities and views represent the diversity of America (and contradict the notion that conservatism is a white, middle-class male phenomenon): from moderate conservative Sarah Cupp to Tomi Lahren, Dana Loesch, Sara Gonzales and Michelle Malkin; from Ted Cruz, Ben Shapiro and Mark Levin to the far-right hipster Gavin McInnes.

In keeping with the growing radicalness and fanaticism of the online political conversation, the nu-troglodytes of American conservative entertainment live somewhere on the fringes of conspiracy theory, extreme polemic and chat forum trolling. Ironically, the mainstream sees *them* as conspirators, maliciously promoting 'fake news' to assuage bruised egos and for financial gain. There's some truth to this, but the full picture is more complex.

I think the appeal of outrageously conspiratorial entertainment masquerading as news is down to three things:

1. **The Online Disinhibition Effect.** The academic John Suler identified six factors that can make people behave more nastily online than they would in what was then considered the 'real' world. These six factors are that people can't see one another, don't know one another and don't have to communicate in real time, and as a result have to imagine what others intend and can pretend that being nasty is just part of a game, particularly because there are no authority figures to police what they say or write.
2. **The increase in PR-placed stories and content marketing in the mainstream news.** The rise of 24/7 news and the decrease in people's willingness to pay for it means that journalists are under greater pressure to produce more frequent stories and that newsrooms have to rely to an ever-greater extent on advertisers. A former journalist once told me that unless a piece of news is truly 'breaking' (for example, a report about a natural disaster), it's more likely than not been placed by a PR agency on behalf of a client. This is no secret, and obviously encourages mistrust of the mainstream media.
3. **Online social networks encourage ideological bubbles.** Once upon a time, social media sites wrote algorithms that made us see more of what we like in our news feeds, filtering out content that it had learned we don't like. Nowadays, we choose to create these online bubbles for ourselves. In these bubbles, it feels good to be outraged by the other side's behaviour and to rant about it with people who feel the same as we do. These are fertile conditions for conspiracy.

These changes align well with commercial interests because focusing on a 'genre' drives profitability as people choose brands that they know will offer new twists on themes they're familiar with and enjoy. Conservative channels consistently generate huge profits, and this strategy is increasingly pursued by other networks – from CNN to ESPN, Disney to Al Jazeera. In 1988 Roger Ailes wrote: 'In this video age we're all broadcasters. We transmit our own programmes. We receive ratings from our audiences. We've been absorbed by the medium of television, and now we are part of that medium'. Thirty years later, never has this been truer. All of us, whether we like it or not, are mighty troglydyti.

What can we learn from Case story 5?

These days, most large companies use some form of enterprise social network (ESN) to encourage employee connection and collaboration, and as a platform for internal communications. Pearson launched their ESN in 2011 and people began creating personal profiles and starting groups based around professional and personal interests. There were groups for cross-company projects, homepages for specific teams and forums like 'Pearson cyclists'. Around this time I was a comms manager, and I found it infuriating that I couldn't get people to engage as enthusiastically with projects on the ESN as they would with personal-interest groups. The top-ranking pages for interactions were always for things like 'lunchtime runners' and '*Star Wars* nerds'. It was at least a little comforting to know that it wasn't just me who faced this challenge. Most comms managers across Pearson also found it hard, and I've subsequently discovered that it's a challenge people at a lot of companies face.

People are obviously emotionally invested in personal interests like cycling, running and *Star Wars*. Part of the fun is being subjective – having an opinion about it. Instinctively, people with common interests debate one another, give outlandish polemics and parody themselves or others. Being involved in a debate or creating a parody or delivering a polemic can be stimulating, but it's also entertaining for the audience of those debates, parodies and polemics. The passionate sharing of opinions creates a scene that attracts other people who also share that general interest. In these special-interest groups attempts at objectivity are usually ignored.

The problem for organisations is that, being inherently political places, objectivity is the default setting for most activity and associated communications. Objectivity is ineffective for two reasons:

1. **It's boring.** Objectivity isn't entertaining because it resists emotionality. But people gravitate to things if they feel an emotional connection. In the workplace, where people are busy with projects and dealing with their colleagues, and talking to their friends and families, and engaging with content online (on their phones if not their desktops), it's easy to ignore boringly objective but strategically important projects.
2. **It's bewildering.** Objectivity resists a narrative because narrative is emotive. But people experience and explain the world as stories, and if we can't pick out a storyline in something we're reading, watching or hearing we get confused. When we get confused we get frustrated and turn our attentions to things that are more satisfying.

There's a great anecdote in Chip and Dan Heath's book *Made to Stick* about the importance of finding an emotionally arresting headline in a news story to get people's attention and help them understand the facts. Nora Ephron was a journalist who became the Hollywood screenwriter who penned classic rom-coms like *When Harry Met Sally* and *Sleepless in Seattle*. When she was in journalism school, her class was given an assignment to write a headline for an announcement that all teachers at a school would be attending a training course on new teaching methods, delivered by prestigious academics. Every student tried to condense the facts into a single sentence. The teacher read them and dismissed all of their attempts, saying, 'the lead to the story is, "*There will be no school next Thursday*"'. Years later, Ephron remembered it as a defining moment in her education:

In that instant I realised that journalism was not just about regurgitating the facts but about figuring out the point. It wasn't enough to know the who, what, when, and where; you had to understand what it meant. And why it mattered.

Everyone connects immediately and emotionally with the announcement that there'll be no school on Thursday: teachers who think 'the school actually *cares* about our professional development, and won't it be great to have some *freedom* from those kids?!'; the schoolkids who think 'a *sacred* day free from *oppression* by our teachers!'; and their parents who groan 'great. Now I've got to find someone to keep my kids away from *harm* while I'm at work'. In the United States, with its long-standing orthodoxy of objectivity in the news, conservatives like Bill Buckley, Rush Limbaugh and Roger Ailes deliberately eschewed that, using subjectivity to help conservatives make sense of current events and to better educate them in the conservative political curriculum. It was *sacrilegious* to liberals, but it was also really smart.

In the paragraph above, the words I've put in italics express strong emotion because they connect to our moral foundations. According to the psychologist Jonathan Haidt, all morality, regardless of different cultural and ethnic heritages, is based on six universally recognisable foundations. Humans judge good and bad behaviour against each of these moral foundations:

1. **Care/Harm:** We like to care for other living things, and dislike seeing people harm others. Kindness is good, cruelty is bad.
2. **Fairness/Cheating:** Justice and rights are important to everyone. Recognising people' rights is good; abusing those rights is bad.
3. **Loyalty/Betrayal:** Humans easily form groups and part of what keeps those groups together is commitment. Doing our bit to keep those groups together is good, while undermining those groups is bad.
4. **Authority/Subversion:** Part of what makes society work is its structure and the institutions that keep that structure in place. Obeying the rules of those institutions is good, disobeying them is bad, especially if by disobeying them we harm others.
5. **Liberty/Oppression:** For as much as we like rules and the institutions that keep them, we hate it when others prevent us from doing things we should be able to do. Freedom is good, bullying is bad.
6. **Sanctity/Degradation:** Every society has its totems and taboos, stemming from our hopes and aspirations and our instinct to survive. Noble behaviour is good, disgusting things are bad.

The headline 'There will be no school on Thursday' works because the mental associations it gives for teachers, parents and schoolkids connect to these moral foundations. American conservatives understand moral psychology better than liberals and have used that understanding to their advantage to craft slogans and messages that go straight for the gut. In my experience, business leaders are a bit like liberals – they have an irrational commitment to rational communication and as such regularly fail to engage their people with their change plans. The six moral foundations, however, are a fantastic reference for when you're trying to find a way to turn a bland, rational message into something more entertaining.

If you've followed the guidance from Case story 4, you'll have written a 'back to the future' vision for your change programme. As you read back over it, you can probably see how you've unconsciously referenced some of these moral foundations. However, as you embark on the difficult process of change, you can't just keep repeating your change vision. You'll need different messaging content for different groups of people, at different stages in the programme, and for different comms formats. You need to motivate people to debate, parody and polemicise around issues relevant to your change programme while mitigating the risks we're all familiar with around online behaviour – rancour, conspiracy and ideological stubbornness. Essentially, you need a programme of entertainment that serves the change vision without being a repeat of it.

To get started, write down the suspicious questions or outright objections you've encountered from people when you revealed your change vision. With reference to the moral foundations framework, identify the moral and emotional issues that underpin the suspicious questions or objections you've faced. Focus on the language that people used when they asked those questions or stated their objections – specific words could clue you in to the correct moral foundations. For example, say your change vision involves setting your people free so that they can experiment with new ideas that will allow them to better fulfil their creative urges (i.e. simplifying a process by getting rid of unnecessary sign-off procedures and flattening your team's organisational structure). Different responses from people suggest different moral concerns at play:

Suspicious question/objection	Moral/emotional underpinning
'Doesn't this risk lower-quality products getting into the hands of customers?'	Care/Harm
'It took us years to perfect this process and I'm concerned that if we undo it we'll take a step backwards.'	Authority/Subversion
'I love this process – it helps us work together as a team and I think you just want to change it to cut costs.'	Sanctity/Degradation

Now write down your counterarguments – one for each of the moral foundations you need to address. Again, pay attention to the language you use – make it authentically you, but unashamedly subjective and moral/ emotional. For example:

Suspicious question / objection	Possible counterargument
'Doesn't this risk lower-quality products getting into the hands of customers?'	*'That's an important concern. I'd like to set up a constructive debate that we can all take part in, to discuss what our customers care most about in terms of our products and how we can best take care of them.'*
'It took us years to perfect this process and I'm concerned that if we undo it we'll take a step backwards.'	*'I have a polemical response to that. This company has been run like a police state for the past however many years and we've all been well indoctrinated. I can't say my knees aren't quaking a little bit myself at the challenge of smashing some of our longest-standing institutions but I'm also pretty excited about it.'*
'I love this process – it helps us work together as a team and I think you just want to change it to cut costs.'	*'I love you guys too. There's something almost holy about what we do here and I really don't like the idea of being the devil who goes around breaking the halos over everyone's head. Which is why I'm asking you to help me do it, so it isn't such a lonely task. I'm just kidding! But seriously, I think we have an opportunity to reach a higher state if we do this change properly.'*

From here, there are all sorts of ways you can bring these counterarguments to life via different tactics to entertain and engage your people. We'll look at some of these tactics in Case story 6.

CASE STORY 6

Channels

Commandment

Use your communications channels inventively to keep people focused on achieving your change vision.

If you're not from America the first thing you ever know of it is usually to do with its commercial culture. As a child in the mid 1980s, for me that went something like:

First, Mickey Mouse and Disney films
Then, McDonalds and Coca Cola
And then, Michael Jackson and Madonna songs

But the first things you're *taught* about America go something like this:

Christopher Columbus discovered America in the Middle Ages
It was a wild place, and cowboys with guns fought Indians with spears
Black people were slaves but there was a war and the slaves were freed

As the picture comes into focus you learn that it was 'the South' where they kept slaves and, even as a child, you intuitively know that slavery was a horrible thing. As America, with all its amazing arts and culture, starts to become more beguiling, the South takes on an ever-greater shade of evil. Everything bad you've ever heard about in the US seems to happen in the South, even if it didn't. That's the unforgiving power of the legacy of slavery. History is written by the winners and as Henry Eichel, a writer for the North Carolina paper the *Charlotte Observer*, says: 'The South is the only part of the United States ever thoroughly defeated and humiliated in war.'

The cultural legacy of defeat and humiliation in the American Civil War starts to seep through via books, film and music in the school curriculum. *To Kill A Mockingbird, Mississippi Burning*, Delta blues, gospel, old school country & western: everything about the South seems so *sad*. Writers like William Faulkner, Flannery O'Connor and Tennessee Williams fused that potent mix of darkness and melancholy so evocatively that critics created a genre of fiction to describe it: Southern Gothic. Today, Southern Gothic is a globally popular multi-media genre, with writers like Cormac McCarthy and the movies that have been made from his books (*The Road, No Country for Old Men*), TV shows (*Walking Dead, True Detective*), video games (Resident Evil: Biohazard, Outlast II), comic books (*Preacher, Southern Bastards*) and music (Lucinda Williams, Johnny Cash's American Recordings). Whether you've been there or not, the *idea* of the South is familiar to most of us.

On my first and only trip to the Deep South I felt a little apprehensive. I had visions of being the lone guest at creaky antebellum hotels run by thin and sombre Calvinists, with flickering lights on the wall and the scratchy sound of, say, Patsy Cline's 'Crazy' playing repeatedly on an ancient record player, drifting down from the eaves of the house late at night. We drove east out of Austin, Texas and when we got to Louisiana the roads were as bad as we'd been told they would be, the result of the federal government withholding much-needed highway maintenance funds in the 1980s and 1990s because the state refused to raise the legal drinking age to 21. Jackson, Mississippi was eerily quiet, particularly near the state capitol building where the golden eagle atop its dome faces south, legendarily in defiance of Washington DC (very much so a legend – it's not true). The most unsettling moment came in Tennessee when I read the map wrong and we ended up on a flat plain in the middle of nowhere, a long way from the Blue Ridge Mountains, our intended destination. We stopped at a roadside bar and an aggressive young drunk promised us some fun. I think he meant well, but he led us to a rural brothel down a dirt road where women in tight dresses peered out from the porch, anticipating punters as our car headlights bounced towards them. We did an adrenalin-fuelled U-turn and drove as fast as we could into Kentucky, where a highway patrol officer stopped me for speeding.

6.1 *Southern eagle on the State Capitol, Jackson, Mississippi*

I'd been primed from an early age with ideas of a richly exotic South and it was disorienting to find that it wasn't much like that at all. What was most striking was just how visibly poor it is. You don't stay in crumbling old hotels – you stay in dingy motels. You don't eat grits in roadside shacks – you eat shitty fast food in all-too-familiar chains. The countryside was often littered with trash and the cities were shabby. The music on Beale Street in Memphis didn't conjure Southern Gothic in the way that the *idea* of Memphis music does, because Southern Gothic is romantic and Beale Street was depressingly dilapidated. The South remains the poorest region of the country by some distance. Southern Gothic, which in reality has nothing much to do with the South, is a multi-billion-dollar industry.

Today, we're exposed to more ideas about the character of places and things than ever before. Everything strives to be a brand – to control its own narrative. To keep up with the world of ideas that we expose ourselves to we have to find ways of deciding whether to believe them. We ask our friends what they think, we look to so-called experts for guidance, we look for video or photographic evidence. The more channels through which we hear a consistent message, the more likely we are to believe it. Entertainment, because it's narrative led, helps us make sense of the way we feel about new ideas. Entertainment like Southern Gothic that uses a variety of channels to communicate similar themes is even more persuasive.

So, the commandment for this case story is: Use your communications channels inventively to keep people focused on achieving your change vision.

REPOSITIONING THE REPUBLICANS

Lee Atwater's life was Southern Gothic writ large. At five years old he watched his baby brother burn to death after pulling a deep fat fryer over. Unable to ever shake the memory of his brother's agonised screams, Atwater threw himself into politics with all the manic energy that characterised his life. He cut his teeth in the notoriously tough politics of South Carolina before masterminding Reagan's 1984 landslide victory and George

H. W. Bush's successful campaign in 1988. Bush rewarded him by making him chairman of the Republican National Committee. By 1991, he was dead of a brain tumour at 40 years old. Paying tribute, Atwater's protégé, Karl Rove, remembered, 'Lee Atwater was part myth, part showman and part political mastermind. He was one of the most unique people I've ever met in my life.' B. B. King, with whom he played the blues, said simply that he felt like he'd lost a son.

At first glance, Atwater's legacy as a pioneering Republican strategist was as confounding as Rush Limbaugh's rise to king of the conservatives. But America in the seventies was changing, and over the course of 15 short years Atwater, as Southern as a boy could be, would change forever how the party functioned. He re-oriented it towards younger voters and rode rough-shod over accepted practices of political communication.

In the South, politics was sport and entertainment, meaning it was hard and competitive, and bombastic and outrageous. Atwater loved professional wrestling for the way it combined combat sport and cartoonish entertainment, and for the way smaller guys could fight dirty, without disapproval, in order to beat bigger opponents. In wrestling, a small guy like Lee could sneak up behind a Goliath and smash him on the head with a chair while the referee wasn't looking, and the crowd would cheer. To Lee, the parallels with politics were obvious: 'Atwater felt that wrestling was the only honest sport because it was so obviously dishonest. What's there to entertain and distract is what counts,' says journalist Joe Conason.

Upon joining the College Republicans, Atwater began experimenting with the tactics that would turbocharge his career. He wrote a comedy newsletter to help get his friend elected class president and realised that people wanted to be featured in the paper. They were just like him: they craved attention. He began asking good-looking fraternity boys and sorority sisters to persuade members of the opposite sex to join the Young Republicans. When Republican politicians came to town to speak, he'd strategically place his frat brothers in the audience and get them to stand and

applaud even if the talk wasn't particularly inspiring, so that their enthusiasm would influence others to do the same. It was thrilling because it
worked. Atwater had found his calling: 'I feel that I have an intuitive grasp
of the political scene', he once said. 'I can't always cite stats but I can feel
what's in the air'.

He finagled a role for himself as a low-level staffer in the Reagan White
House in 1980 and seized his opportunity to apply his ideas at the top level
of the national stage during Reagan's re-election campaign in 1984. Atwater's two big ideas were not all that original:

1. Like Rush Limbaugh, he felt that the growing importance of media
    in people' lives meant politics would have to become more
    entertaining.
2. Like Kevin Phillips, he sensed that if the Republicans could be suc-
    cessfully repositioned as the party of the South, they could dominate
    national politics.

Atwater's unique insight was that these two ideas were intimately connected. If the first proved true, the second was almost a fait accompli:
political entertainment would help make America more conservative.
His reputation was earned in the way he used comms channels to prove
this concept. When Roger Ailes launched Fox News he did so with the
confidence that Lee Atwater had already laid the groundwork for its
success.

Atwater understood that political entertainment was a by-product of
whatever battle was currently being fought. Entertaining vignettes could
be created by giving the 'inside story' on a minor victory such as a well-re-
ceived response by the Republican candidate in a televised debate or a poll
suggesting that Atwater's candidate was in the lead. As a TV talking head,
Atwater drew viewers by explaining why he thought a particular victory
was achieved and then 'strategising in public' about what his campaign
intended to do next to capitalise on their advantage. Strategising in public
had three obvious benefits:

6.2 *Lee Atwater rocking out with George H. W. Bush*

1. it made for good TV, making the media friendly towards talking heads that gave good airtime;
2. it suggested transparency on the part of the campaign, and intelligence on the part of the talking head who appeared to be thinking coherently on the spot;
3. it allowed the strategist to subtly plant ideas about the opposition and their perceived weaknesses that the audience would internalise.

Behind the scenes, Atwater heavily invested in the Republicans' opposition research capabilities. Opposition research involved trawling through media archives to find information about opposing candidates that would cast them in a bad light. In the eighties, the Democrats' research operation consisted of two researchers, a secretary, and five filing cabinets. In contrast, Atwater had at his disposal 35 'excellent nerds' as he called them, five data processors, and a mainframe computer with hundreds of thousands of cross-indexed entries on big name Democrats. Atwater spent hours poring over 'oppo' clippings so that he could develop negative themes about the other side's candidates. Atwater fed these themes to hungry journalists and used telemarketing campaigns to seed ideas directly with voters. For example, a telemarketer might ask, 'if you knew that such-and-such candidate was a womaniser who had cheated on his wife on numerous occasions, would you support them while in office?' Leading questions like this encouraged voters to draw emotional conclusions along the lines of 'if the Democratic candidate is a womaniser then how can he be trusted in office?'

Atwater also knew how to use symbolism to win voters. 'Lee understood the power of image and how American symbols resonate with a lot of southerners,' says his former aide, Tucker Eskew. 'Democrats to this day scratch their head and can't believe that people vote against their own interest by supporting these Republicans, but the fact is that proud patriotism transcends money'. Atwater took gleeful inspiration from cult horror movies that traded on the North's fear of the South, like *Two Thousand Maniacs!* in which a town of yee-hawing rednecks massacre a group of stranded northerners during a Confederate celebration. His political messages deliberately exploited Yankee caricatures of the South as backwards and uncivilised, eschewing policy detail in favour of emotional entertainment. 'In the South that's called slow-playin' 'em', his old friend, Rich Peterson, drawls. 'Bein' a slow talker and easygoin' – a lot of northerners perceive that as bein' not very bright. Suck them in and you end up runnin' all over 'em'. Northern elites were caught napping, and responded with bluster and outrage. Howard Fineman, an editor at *Newsweek*, thought Atwater was borderline feral: 'Lee sometimes reminded me of a wolverine, sorta chewing through the plywood. He had a vaguely marsupial look about him, always sniffing the air.' Yet in the days before social media enabled hyper-specific messaging, a strategist had to have a good feel for voters, particularly those who were undecided about which candidate to choose. In this, Atwater was in his element. 'If I've done an innovative thing it's consciously having this working formula which has proved invincible in every campaign,' he bragged.

To become a national party that could command the Sunbelt, the Republicans also had to get out of the country club. 'If the Grand Old Party stayed kinda grand and old it wasn't going to be much of a party. It had to go young,' commented Tucker Eskew. For Atwater, it was radical ideas about the opportunities of the future that mattered to the baby-boom generation. He spelled it out in a think-tank speech to aspirational young Republicans at the peak of his career: 'When you move from an industrial age into the communications and information age, you've got two forces working simultaneously that are very important – a cultural values revolution and a technology revolution. They add up to a "new synthesis".' He was right about the direction of travel. By 1989, a year after helping George H. W. Bush win the presidency, 54% of Republicans were under 40. The Republicans had been successfully repositioned.

FUTURISTIC CONSERVATISM

Newt Gingrich, who took up the mantle for transforming the Republican Party following Lee's death, was a different kind of Southerner. Where Atwater was manic and extroverted, Gingrich was bookish and cerebral. Where Atwater came from a long lineage of rural Carolinians, Gingrich was a transplant to suburban Georgia from a broken home in Pennsylvania and a restive adolescence on US army bases in Western Europe. What they had in common was an opportunistic conservatism that was attuned to the promises of futuristic technology.

Gingrich and Atwater were both fans of Alvin Toffler, the futurist whose books documented how Western cultures were changing as a result of the transformation from an industrial economy to an information age. Ever the pragmatist, Atwater focused on the bottom-line impact of the 'new synthesis' of cultural and technological revolution: 'Alvin Toffler's third wave is more than just computers and high technology – it's entrepreneurialism, offering new freedom and independence to the individual.' For Gingrich, the impact was more profound. As a fifteen-year-old he'd visited the World War I battle-field of Verdun in north-east France, where the heaping skeletal remains of 130,000 soldiers are littered behind glass encasements in the gothic ossuary. In his 1984 book *Window of Opportunity*, he confided that 'twenty-five years after I visited Verdun, I can still feel the sense of horror and reality which overcame me then. It is the driving force which pushed me into history and politics and moulded my life.' For Gingrich, it was the marriage of capital-ism and the democratic promise of technology that would affirm the United States as the world's leading superpower. He thought grandiosely, writing of the 'sweeping dreams' by which societies shape themselves and the 'quantum leap in living standards that our children can achieve from the information revolution'. But just as the World Wars had savaged Europe's global lead-ership, there was a risk that America would not achieve its promise. Alvin Toffler warned of the 'psychological disease' of 'future shock', a 'dizzying disorientation brought on by the premature arrival of the future'. Traditional conservatives preached that moral turpitude would bring America to ruin. Libertarians claimed that an unbalanced national budget would do for the country, while neoconservatives argued that foreign policy weakness would undermine America's international influence. Gingrich synthesised the three disparate lines of thought to conclude that liberalism was exacerbating the risk of future shock for the majority of Americans.

As with Atwater, it was Gingrich's sense of the South that shaped him. As an assistant history professor at West Georgia College he created a course on Alternative Lifestyles and taught seminars in a circle on the grass, with more counterculture students in his class than any other professor. But Atlanta was the centre of the New South and Gingrich's outlook began to change, as the city became a manufacturing and technology metrop-olis with a fast-growing suburban middle class. Gingrich introduced a Future Studies programme, where he taught the media, management and strategy theories of Marshall McLuhan, Peter Drucker and Herman Kahn. He invited Alvin Toffler in as a guest lecturer, with whom he struck up an enduring friendship. In 1978, he entered Congress as the Republican Representative for the affluent northern suburbs of Atlanta, an area that came to be nicknamed 'Newtland' as his star rose and its dominant political beliefs were popularised by Gingrich: low taxes, anti-labour union, strong work ethic, commitment to family and community. Immediately, Gingrich set his sights on becoming Speaker of the House of Representatives.

6.3 *Gingrich in Korea, looking north*

At this stage, it's worth interrupting the narrative with a brief aside about the role of Congress in the American political system. There are three branches of the federal government:

1. the executive branch: the office of the President
2. the judicial branch: The Supreme Court
3. the legislative branch: Congress.

Congress, both for its structure and its role, is closest to the American people. The two chambers in Congress are the Senate and the House of Representatives. Each state, regardless of its population size, has two senators. The number of representatives each state gets is correlated to its population (the bigger the population, the more representatives it gets). Representatives are often referred to as congressmen and women, and each one represents a geographical district within a state. As such, they are as beholden to a local community as a member of Congress gets. One of the most important things that Congress does is guide how the federal government raises national revenues and spends public funds. Within Congress, it's only the House that can initiate this legislation (though it must be ratified by the Senate to become law). The President of the Senate is the Vice President of the United States. The Speaker of the House, on the other hand, is voted into the role by their fellow representatives. Gingrich's ambition was not just pragmatically achievable but also strategic, given the post holder's directive over national finances and authority over representatives with their grassroots-community focus.

As a junior congressman, Gingrich was a poor legislator but a successful organiser who knew how to generate noise around his ideas. He had an almost-commercial view of the electorate, treating them more like customers to be cultivated than voters to whom he needed to appeal. Together with other radical young House Republicans, he created the Conservative Opportunity Society (COS), whose name was carefully field-tested to ensure it resonated with their audience. The clue was in the word 'Opportunity', which dovetailed with Atwater's instincts about how to attract younger voters to the conservative Republican cause. COS created a legislative platform built around 'magnets': ideas that would attract swing voters to a future-focused conservative agenda, with a special focus on tax-reduction and state-level control of how taxes were spent. They also used technology to pioneer what we would now call a political echo chamber.

One of Alvin Toffler's ideas had a particularly big impact on Gingrich's thinking:

> Political democracy, by incorporating larger and larger numbers in
> social decision-making, facilitates feedback. And it is precisely this

feedback that is essential to control. To assume control over accelerated change, we shall need more advanced – and more democratic – feedback mechanisms.

Gingrich's entrance to Congress coincided with the launch of C-SPAN, the public service broadcast network that televises the proceedings of Congress. COS used C-SPAN to communicate their ideas directly to the public, avoiding the filter of the often hostile mainstream media. In the early mornings and early evenings when the House chamber was empty, COS members would deliver uninterrupted one-minute monologues direct-to-consumer via the C-SPAN cameras. Rush Limbaugh was often listening in and would put these arguments to his audience as well, using his talent for translating policy into lay terms to build support for conservative ideas. To complete the feedback loop, Gingrich and co. could gauge the public response from call-ins to Limbaugh's station, and use these insights to advance or block legislation in line with popular sentiment.

Gingrich took this a step further when he took over the chairmanship of the Republican politician-training organisation GOPAC in 1986. C-SPAN allowed the twelve members of COS to reach a large audience, serving as a mouthpiece of sorts for the radical Republican HQ. GOPAC was an opportunity to scale up by franchising the message to loyal foot soldiers. The use of multiple channels reinforced the importance of the ideas they were spreading. Gingrich recorded instructional cassettes that explained how Republican candidates could 'talk like Newt'. Candidates would listen to the tapes in their cars as they drove from one campaign stop to another, practising as they listened (sample transcript: 'You cannot maintain civilisation with twelve-year-olds having babies, fifteen-year-olds shooting each other, seventeen-year-olds dying of AIDS, and eighteen-year-olds getting a high school diploma they can't read').

GOPAC political director Tom Morgan also wrote an aide memoire that was distributed to Republican candidates. *Language: A Key Mechanism of Control* outlines the 'optimistic positive governing words' that Republicans should use when talking about conservative ideas, and contrasts them with a list of negative words they should use when talking about liberal policies. Here are a few examples:

Optimistic Positive Governing Words	Contrasting Words
Courage	Betray
Dream	Bizarre
Freedom	Coercion
Opportunity	Disgrace
Tough	Pathetic
Unique	Status quo

The instructional tapes were so effective that they are now in the Library of Congress' National Recording Registry of recordings with historical significance. Together with the GOPAC memo, they remain a powerful and relevant blueprint for teaching people how to use language as a political weapon.

Gingrich assumed speakership of the House in 1992. He briefed pollster Frank Luntz to conduct focus groups every ten days to ask voters what would entrench their commitment to conservatism. From these focus groups came the conviction that five issues were of greatest concern to Americans: debt, welfare, bureaucracy, taxes and spending. These five issues formed the basis of Gingrich's master plan, the Contract with America, which was notable more for its symbolism than its success. Gingrich co-wrote the document with his deputy, Dick Armey, who would go on to have a key role in the Tea Party movement fifteen years later. The signing ceremony on the steps of the Capitol leant heavily on the iconography of the Constitution and the American Revolutionary War in much the way that the Tea Party later did. Though most of its proposed legislation died on the Senate floor, it did help the Republicans win, for the first time in 40 years, control of both the Senate and the House in the 1994 midterm elections.

Icarus-like, Gingrich eventually crashed and burned, resigning the speakership when Republican representatives mutinied in protest at the party's poor performance in the 1998 midterms. Still, his legacy had scorched the political-media complex. Just as Fox News adopted Lee Atwater's ideas about political entertainment as a format, so too did they take the nascent conservative echo chamber that Gingrich kick-started to new heights. Today, rank and file conservative politicians, particularly Republican representatives who are building their careers, can develop close relationships with Fox, who'll give them airtime and endorse their election campaigns if they agree to back ideas that the network champions. Special interest groups that support conservative ideas can pay to promote their concerns via Fox News Issues – a forum for native advertising that plants key messages with viewers with the hope that they remember them, talk about them, and take them to heart. With the arrival of social media and the election of Barack Obama in 2008, the portion of Fox News viewers who got their news from sources other than Fox dropped from 30% to just 2%. Whatever holes there had been in the echo chamber were sealed.

What can we learn from Case story 6?

Change is contentious because there are always alternative courses of action. Some people will say 'let's just continue as we are', and no matter how much you believe that to do that would be tantamount to the organisation rolling over and dying, you can't prove conclusively that they're wrong. Others will say 'I have a better idea', and again, you can't determine for sure that their ideas are worse. You're all talking about the future, and the future is unknowable. Case stories 4 and 5 in this section of the book, 'Communicating change', were about creating a strong argument that *your* way forward is the best option to choose:

Case story 4: Write a 'back to the future' change narrative based on common aspirations of your people to get them to see that the change will benefit them personally.

Case story 5: Create emotive entertainment comms that motivate people by appealing to their moral foundations. Use what you know of their worldviews to craft emotionally intelligent responses to the concerns they raise.

Implicit in the commandments from Case stories 4 and 5 is the idea that you're in control of the message. Most of the time you are – but not always.

There are multiple channels for communication within an organisation, but each fits into one of two categories:

1. broadcast channels
2. feedback channels.

Here are some of the common examples of each that most organisations have at their disposal:

Broadcast channels	Feedback channels
Written word (e.g. emails, blogs, FAQs)	Presentation Q&A sessions
Video	Staff surveys
Presentation talks (e.g. staff briefings, webinars)	Enterprise Social Network (e.g. staff personal blogs, comments sections beneath your broadcast blogs or video)
	Meetings

Clearly, change leaders can control the broadcast channels, but not necessarily the feedback ones. Understandably, many leaders approach using feedback channels with trepidation, for fear of being challenged by a peer who thinks the organisation should go with their change idea instead, or taking a difficult question from someone who's been affected by your change plan. Lee Atwater and Newt Gingrich were experts at taking these kinds of obstacles in their stride and turning them to their advantage. Their inventive use of broadcast and feedback channels in entertaining ways helped make their ideas and arguments more valid in the eyes of their audiences.

Here's how you can apply their tactics, with a specific emphasis on feedback channels.

Magnets. Look back at all your work so far – your profiles of your people and their worlds, your leadership persona, your change vision and rebuttals to people' concerns and objections. Make a list of all the benefits that you believe your change programme will deliver for your people (NOT for the organisation). These are your 'magnets'. It's well understood that when responding through feedback channels you should 'stick to the script' – the script being your key messages. In this case, your key messages are your magnets. They're magnets because they should pull people towards getting on board with your change vision. When refining your magnets, pay careful attention to the moral foundations I covered in Case story 5. The better the magnets speak to the moral foundations that are important to your people, the more magnetic they'll be.

Opposition research. Magnets cover your side of the argument. But what about the other sides – the people who argue that the organisation should remain unchanged, or should take a different change path? This is where you need to do your opposition research. Look for examples of other organisations like yours that have done nothing, or have chosen alternative change paths that haven't worked out well. Ignore how badly these choices impacted the organisation and write down instead how it affected those organisations' employees. Again, put the impact on employees in terms that your people care about at an emotional level. It's not enough to say, '… and so many people were made redundant as a result of that organisation's poor choices'. It's much better to say, for example, 'a significant number of people who lost their jobs were what I call multi-stakeholder managers – knowledgeable, dedicated employees with lots of dependants such as children at university and their own ageing parents. The organisation promised these people that the change path they'd decided upon would work out well for them. The organisation's bad choices left these people high and dry.'

Language. I've made the point ad nauseam that language is massively important. It's particularly powerful if you use strong, positive words to promote your argument and equally strong contrasting words to frame alternative options and their likely negative outcomes. Read through the list of words in the GOPAC memo: it's remarkable how most of them hew so closely to the six moral foundations covered in Case story 5. Regardless of the focus and goals of your change plan, the GOPAC memo words are a good place to start as a reference for the language to use in your communications. From there, make a list of other positive words and contrasting words that are relevant to your people. Use them.

Symbolism and drama. Look again at your 'back to the future' vision and magnets. What imagery would complement what you're trying to communicate? You want this imagery to be simple, strong and dramatic. Think about historic and future-oriented symbolism – a revenant of the important past or a harbinger of the promising future. Keep a log of these images. When you next have a presentation Q&A session, put one of these images up on a screen behind you, as a subtle reminder of the promise you'll deliver.

Strategising in public. This is the ultimate in thinking on your feet when answering difficult questions, and requires you to draw on all the above channel tactics: framing your magnets in positive, symbolic language and drawing on your opposition research to negate alternative courses of action in dramatic fashion. If you're prepared, you'll find strategising in public easier than you think. Essentially, what you're doing is telling people a story about your thought process in order to add credibility to your argument. Not in a long-winded, self-indulgent way, but in an engrossing, provocative way. For example:

Self-indulgent:	'I was lying awake at night struggling to work out what the best way forward is. I dug deep inside myself, and came up with my change vision.'
Engrossing:	'I was watching a show on TV, where two people were gossiping intensely. It struck me how animated and engaged they were. I asked myself, "what do people gossip about?" The answer: intrigue about other people, and that intrigue helps them decide whether they're different or similar to those people. That got me thinking about you lot – us, as a team – who are we, what do we want? That's how I came up with this change vision.'

PART III
Leading change

CASE STORY 7
Misfits

Commandment

Build a change team of people who understand both the cultural surface and its deeps, and who have the skills and behaviours needed to change it.

In 2011, the *Guardian* asked a Dutch journalist, Joris Luyendijk, to demystify the financial services industry for its readers. Luyendijk immersed himself in the culture of the City of London, interviewing employees and blogging those interviews on the *Guardian* website. In *Swimming with Sharks*, a compendium of his interviews and reflections, he offers a vivid analogy of the financial services industry: Planet Finance is an archipelago of enormous institutions, each one an island ecosystem unto itself. The waters around these islands are busy with the traffic of intermediary service providers that keep the archipelago's economy turning. Those of us in what's often called the 'real economy' are in aeroplanes in the skies above and we've discovered that, terrifyingly, the cockpits are empty.

But Luyendijk's real revelation is not that there are no regulatory pilots but that so much of what happens on Planet Finance takes place far beneath the ocean's surface where no one could possibly hope to see, even if they tried. What's happening on the surface tells you little about the real source of action: the ocean deeps.

The surface history of capital markets is a long tale of the democratisation of the market, from the hands of a few banker demigods such as J. P. Morgan in the 19th century, into the hands of the corporations that borrow money in the 20th century, and finally into the hands of the individual small investors who truly provide the market's liquidity in the 21st century.

The whispered truth, however, is that the more lunar pull you have – the closer you are to the centre of action, the greater your financial muscle – the more you can ensure the market swings in your favour. Elite financial institutions use private trading exchanges that are off-limits to the general investing public to influence how the market moves. Luyendijk's analogy is apt: these private trading exchanges are called dark pools, and they're at the heart of the ocean depths of Planet Finance.

No one understood this better than Shelly Maschler, a financial trader from New York's least sexy borough, Staten Island, who put together a ragtag team of misfits that changed the way Wall Street worked forever. Maschler was the archetype of working class Wall Street in the 1980s – a brash, cigar-chomping whisky-barrel of a man who seethed with a hunger to get filthy rich as quickly as possible. Like many a Jewish outsider before him, Maschler resented the way the US banking system was run by and for the benefit of a gentlemen's club of Ivy League-educated WASPs (white Anglo Saxon protestants). His greed was an expression of a belief that it was the democratic right of all Americans to be rich, and motivated by a desire to beat the WASPs at their own rigged game. 'Rules weren't rules for Shelly', said one of his former partners. 'Shelly had a street mentality, and always operated in the bowels of the industry.'

Maschler hired traders in his own self-image: Staten Island kids straight out of high school, or backwater bandits from Queens and the Bronx with dubious degrees from local universities who wouldn't even get to interview at a big bank, never mind work for one. They learned military-level discipline from Maschler's right-hand man, Mike McCarty, who had a volcanic temper that would violently erupt at the slightest deviation from the rules. Maschler taught them how to trade and McCarty kept them in line. But they were successful because a computer whizz kid called Josh Levine had built them a technology platform that would turn the tables on the power brokers of Wall Street.

Like Maschler, Levine was a high-school dropout from a Jewish family who hated the way the financial system worked. Unlike Maschler, he had no

7.1 *Planet Finance, New York City*

desire to be rich (though he would quickly become so). Levine was motivated by an ambition to illuminate the dark pools that drove market prices
for the benefit of the financial elite, enabling the transfer of wealth from the
pockets of ordinary Americans saving for retirement to the bulging port-
folios of the rich. Maschler's best trader, Jeff Citron, took Levine's vision to
up-end Wall Street seriously. Over the course of fifteen years, from 1988
to 2003, Levine and Citron created a series of products that exploited the
inadequacies of deliberately opaque financial technologies to help small-
time investors compete against big financial services firms. As the use of
their online trading platform grew, Levine and Citron hired more renegade
programmers and a management team that subscribed to their libertarian
vision of a totally free market place. In 2002, Island, the platform they'd
built, sold to a Reuters subsidiary, Instinet, for $508 million. In the process,
they revived widespread day trading, helping Middle Americans to invest

in financial markets on more equal terms than at any time since the crash of 1929.

So, the commandment for this case story is: Build a change team of people who understand both the cultural surface and its deeps, and who have the skills and behaviours needed to change it.

THE HIDDEN CURRICULUM

The cultural surfaces of an industry or institution are typically the things it wants to promote about itself. It's the kind of boosterism you find in mission statements, press releases, boilerplate copy, all-staff speeches and the front pages of annual statements. And, of course, change visions – those aspirational narratives that connect the glorious past with a promising future.

The depths of a culture are more complex because they're fragmented and less overtly documented. These cultural depths consist of things like:

- the cultural values of an industry that influence the kinds of people who are routinely hired by organisations within that industry;
- the way employee behaviour and self-identity is influenced by formal expectations, such as dress codes and how people are rewarded for their work;
- the informal expectations of employees, particularly unspoken rules or codes of behaviour that influence how people gain favour and get promoted;
- invisible networks of power within an organisation that reinforce the unspoken rules and codes of behaviour;
- societal perceptions of an industry or organisation that are shaped by history and the nature of the products and services it makes and sells.

The sociologist Philip Jackson coined the term 'hidden curriculum' to define the unintended lessons that students learn in school about how to survive and succeed within the education system and in life. These unintended lessons are taught via the same mechanisms, listed above, that constitute the cultural depths of an industry and/or organisation. Together with the surface features, these hidden factors create a powerful feedback loop between an organisation and/or industry and society at large, along the lines of:

An organisation or industry markets what it is and why what it sells matters …

A customer culture is formed in response to this …

A wider societal perspective is formed based on generally held opinions about the industry and its customers …

Which influences the hiring practices of the industry, and the types of people who want to work for it …

Which continues to shape the way organisations in the industry position themselves and promote their products and services.

The hidden curriculum of the financial services industry, as Shelly Maschler and Josh Levine understood, is that greed is good because greed is democratic; but greed is a sin, so systemic rules that serve greed have no moral force; therefore, breaking those rules and gaming the system in the name of greed is not just permissible but sort of honourable, too. The more of an insider you are, the more successfully you can break those rules without being penalised for it. To be an insider on Wall Street pays handsomely, and the initiation practices of big banks have been finely tuned to convert smart young outsiders with naïve but nuanced views of the financial services industry into professional foot soldiers and insiders-in-waiting. 'It's not the long hours that kill you – it's the lack of control of the hours. My life doesn't belong to me anymore,' complained a first-year analyst, speaking on behalf of all junior financial analysts. The writer Kevin Roose observed how, after just a few months of working in finance, the personalities of recent graduates began to change on the steady march to insiderhood – increased use of industry jargon, using the communal 'we' when referring to their employers ('we closed a deal on Monday', for example) and dressing more expensively. The intelligent young finance recruits with whom he spoke were good at mental compartmentalisation. They admitted that they thought some of their work was ethically suspect, but it was intellectually stimulating and they lived in fear of fucking it up lest they disappoint superiors they admired, or for fear of being bawled out by bosses they detested.

Change expert John Kotter once wrote, 'Never underestimate the magnitude of the forces that reinforce complacency and help maintain the status quo.' These forces are the hidden curriculum of an organisation and industry, so it stands to reason that to make change happen you first need to quantify and understand the hidden curriculum within your organisation and industry. You then need to put together a team that stands a chance of changing the hidden curriculum. This team will need to have the cultural capital to persuade and influence others and the fortitude to persevere when the going gets tough. For this, they'll need to have experience of the hidden curriculum and a genuine drive to want to change it.

A team of outsiders won't be able to do it: while they may well see the hidden curriculum clearly from a distance, they won't have the experience of dealing with its nuances up close and personal. They're likely to be treated with suspicion by the people who the change affects. They're also likely to be too easily manipulated. A team of insiders won't be able to do it either: they simply have too much to lose to risk dedicating themselves unwaveringly to an ambitious change programme. As insiders, it'll be hard for them to admit that the hidden curriculum is a source of friction that's holding the organisation back (after all, being insiders means they likely benefit from it).

To make lasting change happen you need a team of people who have insider-outsider status, and who have the right mix of relevant technical skills needed to achieve your change vision: a misfit team of pragmatic non-conformists. But where to find them if a powerful hidden curriculum can so reliably turn newly hired outsiders into wannabe insiders and, ultimately, into insiders that resist change?

BEHIND ENEMY LINES

In the mid 20th century, scientists conclusively proved what anti-smoking activists had known for decades: cigarettes kill. The anti-smoking lobby was as old as the cigarette industry itself. Early opponents of cigarette smoking cited its cultural offensiveness and potential for moral ruin as well as its suspected negative impact on health. A spirited 20-year battle in the 1890s and 1910s between pro- and anti-smoking activists waged over the right to smoke in public places. The back-and-forth argument that ensued aided the rise of the cigarette.

As the case for prohibiting smoking in public gathered force, tobacco producers, retailers and smokers themselves launched a counteroffensive to make smoking in public even more permissible. Where once it was accepted that smoking was rightfully banned on 'streetcars' (trams) and in train carriages, the pro-smoking lobby successfully campaigned to overturn those bans. As the 20th century progressed, the industry persuaded car manufacturers and furniture makers to build ashtrays into their products to advance the social permissiveness of smoking. The industry was learning a powerful lesson: public debate helped to normalise the cigarette. The more smoking was talked about, the more acceptable it became.

The hidden curriculum of cigarette smoking was forged by this back-and-forth narrative between the industry and its antagonists that continued for the better part of a century. Anti-smokers used the back-and-forth debate to construct a platform that the industry couldn't be trusted to act in the best interests of the public: in the face of the most damning evidence it refused to concede that smoking was addictive or carcinogenic (in fact, Big Tobacco continued to look for ways to make cigarettes even more addictive in the latter decades of the 20th century). For its part, the tobacco industry created a multi-million-dollar public relations industry of its own dedicated to muddying the waters of science. Cross-industry PR groups like the Tobacco Industry Research Committee and the Tobacco Institute used the anti-smoking lobby's myth-busting efforts to help promote tobacco. The back-and-forth narrative was a constant media story, which created an advertising platform for the industry to remind the public that smoking was a choice that all adults enjoyed. Big Tobacco used its opponents myth-busting activities to propagate its own myths about the rightful place of smoking in the culture at large. As the surface story increasingly became 'smoking kills', the hidden curriculum – 'it's cool, it's adult, it's an all-American exercise in freedom' – was reinforced.

Yet as the anti-smoking lobby gathered force in the 1980s and 1990s, the foundations of the industry's PR obfuscation monolith became increasingly unsteady. Philip Morris, ever the most forward-thinking and agile company amongst its competitors, made the strategic decision to come clean, in effect admitting 'it's true, smoking is deadly'. Part of this new communications strategy was to make the hidden curriculum of smoking a more explicit surface narrative: the right to smoke is an all-American freedom. Another aspect of this strategy was to publicly associate with the company values that had tested well in focus groups. These values were:

- trustworthiness
- caring about consumer health
- a commitment to local communities
- supporting the consumer's right to choose by being more transparent about the risks.

The challenge of doing this was captured in a line of dialogue from the film *The Insider*, about the corporate whistleblower Jeffrey Wigand, a biochemist who went to work for the tobacco firm Brown & Williamson (B&W) after a career in the healthcare industry. Lowell Bergman, the television producer who helps Wigand tell his story of intimidation by B&W, reflects on the culture shock that Wigand must have felt upon his move to Big Tobacco:

> You come from corporate cultures where research, creative thinking, these are core values. You go to tobacco … Tobacco is a sales culture. Market and sell enormous volume. Go to a lot of golf tournaments. The hell with everything else.

To create an image of itself as a caring company that respects consumer autonomy and works for public health, Philip Morris would need partners the public could trust. To find these partners, they'd have to go behind enemy lines to recruit insider-outsiders who could credibly help them change perceptions of the company.

There was some precedent for this. In the 1970s, Big Tobacco and the US Public Health Service had briefly collaborated to explore how less harmful 'light' cigarettes could be designed. In the early 1980s, the US Surgeon General recommended that smokers switch to low-tar cigarettes (they were unaware that Big Tobacco's own research showed that 'light' cigarettes were no less harmful than full-flavour brands because smokers compensated when smoking low-tar cigarettes by drawing harder on the butt). Under their new strategy, Philip Morris partnered with the uber-liberal American Civil Liberties Union (ACLU) to defend the right to smoke in the workplace, and stepped up their courtship of academia to legitimise their new image, funding a variety of professorships and programmes:

- A Philip Morris Professor of Sales at Northern Illinois University
- A Philip Morris Chair in Marketing at Yale
- A Philip Morris Endowed Chair of International Business at Virginia Commonwealth University
- A Philip Morris Professor of Plant and Soil Sciences and a Philip Morris Professor of Management Information Systems at the University of Kentucky, which also hosted the Philip Morris Agricultural Leadership Development Program

Pliable academics were paid to write articles arguing that 'steps being taken to protect against exposure to second-hand smoke constitute an intolerable infringement of basic human liberties', and that laws restricting smoking in public would be 'potentially totalitarian' and 'demeaning' to smokers. Many more were drafted to testify in court on behalf of the company in suits brought by the anti-smoking lobby. This was a lucrative income stream; the Harvard statistician Donald Rubin claimed to have made between $1.5 million and $2 million in the late 1990s for his testimonies. Disgusted that so many of his peers had been so readily co-opted by Big Tobacco, the academic Robert Proctor warned that 'the industry is not just *corrupting* academia; they are also *creating* it'.

With the help of a misfit team of insider-outsiders, Philip Morris shaped a new public narrative that tobacco companies should be no more account-able for smoking-related disease than healthcare providers, police officers, convenience store clerks, schoolteachers and parents. If it was every American's right to choose to smoke, so the argument went, then the focus of anti-smoking efforts should be aimed less at tobacco producers than the figures and institutions of authority that can influence consumers at an individual level. By 2004, 60% of Americans believed that Philip Mor-ris was acting more responsibly than it had in the past, and saw it as more trustworthy than other tobacco companies because it had admitted that there was no safe cigarette and was doing its best to become a respected corporate citizen. In 2008, *Fortune* magazine ranked Philip Morris as the tobacco industry's 'most admired company', scoring 8.4 out of 10 based on factors such as social responsibility, commitment to employees, financial soundness and product quality.

IT PAYS TO BE RADICAL

Philip Morris' successful repositioning was a textbook application of the tactics recommended by its former board member Lewis Powell. In a 1971 memo, Powell outlined how the American business community could protect the free enterprise system from anti-capitalist forces fighting for greater regulation. Powell, a corporate lawyer in Richmond, Virginia who counted the Tobacco Institute amongst his clients, urged for greater busi-ness influence in academia and the media. He also encouraged business to use the courts to secure legal rights for private industry, just as the Civil Rights movement had so successfully done.

Two months after Powell penned the memo, President Nixon nominated him to the Supreme Court. A brief furore ensued when the *Washington Post*

7.2 *Supreme Court Justice Lewis Powell*

published the memo. Journalist Jack Anderson editorialised that Powell's counterrevolutionary views were 'so militant that it raises a question about his fitness to decide any case involving business interests'. A southern Democrat, Powell served as a swing-vote Supreme Court justice until his retirement in 1987. The editorial simply served to widely publicise the existence of the memo, widening its readership and gaining support for its arguments.

The Powell Memorandum proved to American business interests that it pays to be radical. Across the country, a group of cryptography wizards in the lowlands of California's South Bay took note. Silicon Valley, on the cusp of the internet revolution in the early 1990s, had long been populated by anarcho-libertarian thinkers that had come of age in the sixties counterculture. As Lee Atwater had so fruitfully understood, issues of personal freedom were of paramount importance to baby boomers, and none more so than technologists who believed that computer code could be used to outwit the overreach of the federal government. In 1992, businessman Tim May, computer scientist John Gilmore and mathematician Eric Hughes organised a small meeting of like-minded radicals to form the cypherpunks. Their motto was innocuous enough: 'cypherpunks write code'. Their mission was anything but: 'many of us are explicitly anti-democratic and hope to use encryption to undermine the so-called democratic governments of the world,' wrote May in his cypherpunk manifesto, *Cyphernomicon*.

Like Josh Levine on Wall Street, the cypherpunks were self-styled outsiders who aimed to change the system from within. Central to their vision was a belief that an individual has a right to absolute privacy while public bodies, most obviously governments, had *no* right to privacy. In a few short years, cypherpunk members would create prototypes for the kind of online encryption tools and pro-transparency platforms with which we're all familiar today:

- BlackNet, a precursor to WikiLeaks
- b-money, an early example of a cryptocurrency like bitcoin
- Assassination Market, a forum for anonymously contributing to a bounty to have influential people killed and that presaged the rise of dark web black markets like the Silk Road.

Like Lewis Powell and devotees of his memo, the cypherpunks were also unabashed elitists who adopted the language and form of counterculture-style radicalism to build a furtive movement. The 'cypherpunk' name was 'a marketing ploy, to be honest' admitted May. 'A bit like Anonymous wearing the Guy Fawkes masks'. In *Cyphernomicon*, May wrote disparagingly of 'inner-city breeders, non-productive citizens, and the clueless 95%'. The cypherpunks imagined creating a secluded community like the one envisioned by the high priestess of libertarianism, Ayn Rand, in her novel *Atlas Shrugged*, where the world's most productive citizens avoid taxes and pursue greatness. This outlook was shared by another organisation co-founded by John Gilmore, the Electronic Frontier Foundation (EFF). EFF would significantly advance the cypherpunk cause as Silicon Valley bestrode the 21st century.

Gilmore's partners in EFF were fellow cyberlibertarian activists Mitch Kapor, an entrepreneur who developed the first spreadsheet software, and John Perry Barlow, a wealthy countercultural dabbler who, amongst other things, was a long-serving lyricist for hippie band the Grateful Dead. Following a brush with the FBI about online intellectual property theft, the men realised that the US government was clueless as to how to manage and regulate online activity. Recognising that laws would slowly but surely be developed, they founded EFF to advise and guide the development of those laws. Kapor explained their vision in a *Wired* magazine article: 'Private, not public life in cyberspace seems to be shaping up exactly like Thomas Jefferson would have wanted: founded on the primacy of individual liberty and a commitment to pluralism, diversity, and community'. Styling themselves as a hip watchdog group and with the backing of early Silicon Valley luminaries such as Apple's Steve Wozniak and *The Whole Earth Catalog*'s Stewart Brand, EFF secured lobbying sponsorship from a variety of telecoms giants, including IBM, AT&T and Microsoft.

In keeping with their mission to preserve the ideology of the 1960s, EFF recruited Jerry Berman, a lawyer and lobbyist for the American Civil Liberties Union who had led the ACLU Projects on Privacy and Information Technology in the eighties. During his time at ACLU, Berman brokered strategic alliances with lobbying groups in Washington DC who represented traditionally conservative interests, from partnering with the National Rifle Association (NRA) to prevent the Department of Justice collecting arrest data for background checks that would allow them to deny firearms licences, to defending the alcoholic drinks industry and Big Tobacco in fighting efforts to ban them from advertising their products.

Berman spearheaded EFF's development into America's most influential internet lobby that has helped shape the commercial internet. Following Lewis Powell's seminal recommendations, it has funded academics, economists, journalists and privacy organisations, often in collaboration with the influence networks set up by other 'radical rich' libertarians. In keeping with the views of the cypherpunks and its corporate donors, chief among them Google and Facebook, EFF has developed a powerfully simple lobbying message:

> Tech companies privilege people across the world with free access to online tools that have become essential to modern life and personal advancement. They understand user privacy and can be trusted to protect it. Governments want to introduce online regulation so they can access users' private data for social control and monitoring purposes. They can't be trusted so we should resist their efforts.

Of course, a hidden curriculum lurks just beneath the surface. The hidden curriculum of the commercial internet is that the free tools and protection of user privacy are offered by tech companies to individuals in return for their loyalty. To reciprocate, users must accept that companies need easy access to their personal data in order to continue to provide these services. The more data we provide, the more personalised these services can become.

Working through EFF, the world's biggest technology companies have fashioned a hip cultural argument that rephrases Ronald Reagan's Pollyannaish view that the brilliance of the private sector vastly outshines the Cinderella-like role of government. The misfits, they say, have inherited the earth and are making it a better place.

7.3 *Child-friendly EFF poster*

What can we learn from Case story 7?

Putting together a strong change team requires a frank assessment of some daunting realities:

1. the hidden curriculum of your organisation (and possibly industry)
2. the levels of support and resistance inside the organisation for your change goals
3. a fast-changing labour market
4. your headcount budget for recruiting effective insider-outsiders.

Let's look at how to do that frank assessment of each of these realities. Fortunately, if you've been following the commandments for each case story so far, you'll already have gathered a lot of relevant data.

1. The hidden curriculum. Earlier in Case story 7 I identified some of the markers of a hidden curriculum. Here they are again:

- the cultural values of an industry that influence the kinds of people who are routinely hired by organisations within that industry;
- the way employee behaviour and self-identity is influenced by formal expectations, such as dress codes and how people are rewarded for their work;
- the informal expectations of employees, particularly unspoken rules or codes of behaviour that influence how people gain favour and get promoted;

- invisible networks of power within an organisation that reinforce the unspoken rules and codes of behaviour;
- societal perceptions of an industry or organisation that are shaped by history and the nature of the products and services it makes and sells.

I also outlined how the hidden curriculum influences a feedback loop that develops between an organisation/industry and society at large:

- an organisation or industry markets what it is and why what it sells matters …
- a customer culture is formed in response to this …
- a wider societal perspective is formed based on generally held opinions about the industry and its customers …
- which influences the hiring practices of the industry, and the types of people who want to work for it …
- which continues to shape the way organisations in the industry position themselves and promote their products and services.

Use these pointers to document the hidden curriculum of your organisation. Your notes on the culture of your organisation (see Case story 1) and the SITU analysis of your employee personas (see Case story 2) may be helpful to refer to as you do this. Focus on:

- the cultural values of the industry and your organisation
- the kinds of people who are hired by the organisation
- the formal and informal expectations of employees that influence their behaviour
- the invisible networks of power within the organisation (think cliques and niches)
- societal perceptions of the organisation and industry
- the customer culture for your industry.

2. Levels of support and resistance for your change vision. As you look over your answers to the questions about the hidden curriculum of your organisation, ask yourself how each aspect is likely to engender support or resistance to your change plan. Organise these notes in two columns:

Support	Resistance

As you do this, it might be helpful to refer to the 'opposition research' notes you took (see Case story 6), when you were cataloguing why alternative change ideas that your colleagues introduced wouldn't work. Has the hidden curriculum influenced their ideas? How is this likely to contribute to resistance to your ideas as a result? On the flip side, as you revisit your SITU Analysis of employee personas, think about how your ideas for keeping people onside can serve as a foundation of support for your change programme. Finally, include any other indicators of support or resistance.

3. A fast-changing labour market. The organisation needs your change plan because the outside world is ever-changing. That ever-changing world has huge implications for the labour market, which affects all of us. In fact, I'd go as far as to say that there's an overarching, macro-level hidden curriculum for the labour market that influences how people approach working life. Some of the factors shaping this hidden curriculum include:

- job insecurity, as automation and competition fuel the rise of the gig economy at the lower end of the labour market;
- lifelong learning, at all levels of the labour market as a knowledge-led and services-oriented economy require people to learn new skills and upgrade existing ones;
- financial uncertainty, as ageing populations with higher expectations of quality of life than previous generations put pressure on public and private pension provision;
- multi-generation workplaces, as older people delay retirement even as younger workers enter the labour market;
- career variety, as people supplement their income and pursue new passions and interests with side hustles and portfolio careers.

This labour market hidden curriculum is likely to be different depending on geographical market, the type of industry and skill levels of workers, as well as age and stage of life. Consider the people who will be affected by your change plan and identify the most salient factors of the labour market hidden curriculum that apply. Sort them according to whether they could support or encourage resistance to your programme.

4. Recruiting insider-outsiders on a budget. If budget is a constraining factor you'll need to build a team that includes people who already work for the organisation as well as recruiting from outside. Look first at your notes in the 'support' column. When you look down the list, what kind of person – their traits, behaviours and attitudes – embodies the factors you've listed? These are the kinds of people I'd want to recruit from within the company, because you need to build from a position of strength. Make a list of all the people within the organisation who you think could play a role in your change programme who fit the type. Now look at the items in the 'resistance' column. What kind of experiences, skills and perspectives might someone have who could powerfully counter these things that are, essentially, the barriers to the success of your change plan? Make a list of the different places you could find these insider-outsiders, taking inspiration from the stories in this case story. Shape the job roles you need to recruit around the experiences, skills and perspectives you want people to have and, of course, the budget you have available.

Networks

Commandment

Cultivate and use your networks at all levels of your organisation and industry, without letting them co-opt or derail your change plan.

I emptied the Styrofoam cup onto the steaming asphalt of the diner parking lot.

'It's not coffee, it's just black water,' I complained. 'I'll go to Starbucks in Monument Valley'.

I could see the giant rocks in the far distance down the scarred road that connected Arizona to Utah, a straight strip of terra firma across the uneven sea of red desert.

'There won't be a Starbucks. It's a Navajo reservation.' She took a picture of the endless-sameness vista.

'Everywhere touristy in America has a Starbucks,' I joked, with absolute conviction that there would be.

But there was nothing in Monument Valley for tourists except a handful of rudimentary lodgings overlooking the ancient terrain. I was suspicious when our guide, bumping his jeep indiscriminately over the dunes the next day, told us that some of his people lived nomadically out here, with none of the trappings of Western civilisation. He pointed at a parched white animal skeleton, then at an overhanging rock. 'Eat the sheep, build fire, sleep in cave.' I shivered in the heat at the thought of it.

There's nothing as humbling as the American outdoors. Standing in the huge, silent stillness of Monument Valley, or Yosemite National Park, or the Great Salt Lake, you can imagine dying alone and insignificant. There, to commune with nature like the hardiest Navajo is to simply survive it and give thanks for its mercy. It's no surprise why indigenous Americans hold the elements sacred.

For the visitor, the idea of being untethered to anything but the raw earth in the American West is enough to make you stay in the car with the doors locked and the air-conditioning on full blast, stopping at every one-pump gas station you come across for fear of the tank running dry in the dark in the middle of nowhere. Intentionally or not, we give thanks to the foolhardy pioneers who built the networks that make the West now seem conquerable to us all. The business barons who built the roads and created jobs for the unskilled labourers who first populated the region, the wildcatters who found oil and landscaped a petrolhead's paradise, the inventors who put GPS satellites in the sky and pushed the final frontier beyond the Pacific Ocean into cyberspace.

Networks enhance and constrain our lives, often at the same time. There's nothing commercial about Monument Valley, which adds to its beauty but also contributes to the poverty in which so many of the Navajo live. Commerciality would bring jobs and prosperity but ruin the land and compromise the culture. This tension is also at the heart of modern American conservatism, between the libertarian pursuit of wealth and the social conservatives' hankering for a slower, simpler small-town America. Networks have formed between these factions based on the shared values of patriotism, property ownership, self-determination and small government. But these tensions are always there like fault lines in the earth. Nowhere were these tensions clearer than in the 2016 Republican primaries, when the Tea Party candidate Ted Cruz who was backed by 'radical rich' libertarians lost the nomination to Donald Trump. With his Reagan-echoing promise to 'Make America Great Again', Trump won most of the Rustbelt, the Sunbelt and the West – places where working-class communities are dealing with the learned helplessness of decades of joblessness and a squeezed middle class are struggling to meaningfully participate in a changing economy.

8.1 *Monument Valley, Utah*

At an organisational level, American conservatism is extremely adaptive. Its people pragmatically pursue their ideological aims, building networks and coalitions to advance the conservative cause. When they succeed, they look to entrench what's been achieved; when these networks and coalitions fail, they pragmatically splinter and regroup in new formations to pursue new lines of attack. Never do they waver in their mission to defeat modern liberalism and roll back its achievements. If anything, conservatives have become more determined and aggressive in their bid to win as time goes on. Tellingly, this increased conservative belligerence reflects and encourages its supporters' frustrations with the country they love but a society they resent.

So, the commandment for this case story is: Cultivate and use your networks at all levels of your organisation and industry, without letting them co-opt or derail your change plan.

NETWORK EFFECTS

Over the past fifty years, conservative activists have refined two different but complementary methods for making the United States a more conservative country. Both methods grew out of the people and groups that coalesced around Barry Goldwater's reluctant turn in the national political spotlight in the late 1950s and early 1960s. Both methods are also examples of the power of the network effect, where, as more people engage with the conservative cause, the more powerful these networks become. One, a bottom-up approach that advocated that conservatism would be advanced via grassroots activism, grew out of the Young Americans for Freedom (YAF) group, which itself grew out of the Youth for Goldwater group who set up advocacy chapters on university campuses. The second was a top-down approach spearheaded by Paul Weyrich, a young evangelical Goldwater acolyte, who argued that conservatives should reverse engineer the means by which liberals successfully got legislation passed. In Weyrich's view, liberals networked their ideas into law because the cosy corridors of power were so reliably stocked with people whose bible was the liberal consensus. In short order, conservatives needed influential policy-writing foundations, friendly journalists, grassroots groups and politicians on tap and in seamless alignment with one another.

Marvin Liebman, a bohemian teenage communist who was dishonourably discharged from the US Army for being gay, morphed the Youth for Goldwater group into YAF. By this time, Liebman ran publicity for *National Review*. Bill Buckley, eager to cultivate his employee's new group, organised a YAF conference at his estate in Sharon, Connecticut in 1960. Buckley was impressed by what he saw:

What was so striking in the students who met at Sharon is their appetite for power. Ten years ago the struggle seemed so long, so endless, even, that we did not dream of victory. The difference in psychological attitude is tremendous. They talk about *affecting* history; we have talked about *educating* people to want to affect history.

M. Stanton Evans, a young conservative newspaper editor, drafted a short statement of principles for the group on the flight to Connecticut. A number of well-connected establishment figures were present to guide the meeting, including:

New Jersey governor Charles Edison
Novelist and artist John Dos Passos
William Rusher, publisher of *National Review* magazine
Allan Ryskind, publisher of *Human Events* magazine

And among the 100 or so students who attended, some would rise to positions of significant power in other important areas, such as:

Future Ivy League academic Lee Edwards
Future federal judge Paul Niemeyer
Policy wonk and future presidential candidate Howard Phillips
Don Lipsett, founder of conservative networking group the Philadelphia
Society

All signed the resulting Sharon Statement. It combined ideas from each of the three branches of conservative thought – traditionalism, libertarianism and anti-communism – into five overarching principles:

1. individual freedom and the right of governing originate with God
2. political freedom is impossible without economic freedom
3. limited government and strict interpretation of the Constitution
4. the free market system is preferable over all others
5. communism must be defeated, not contained.

The Sharon Statement inspired a response by the New Left when, two years later, the Students for a Democratic Society (SDS) issued the Port Huron Statement. The momentum, however, was with the conservatives. By the mid sixties, YAF membership was at 28,000 while the SDS had just 2,000. Buckley's friend and fierce ideological rival, journalist Murray Kempton, wrote decidedly: 'We must assume that the conservative revival is *the* youth movement of the '60s.'

Opposition to the Vietnam War would temporarily slow the stratospheric growth of youthful conservatism. In Washington DC, a group of newly politicised business leaders and tycoons were ready to take up the baton. They had been inspired to action largely by Lewis Powell's infamous memo to preserve American capitalism. Deftly seizing his moment, Paul Weyrich pressed billionaire Joseph Coors, heir to the beer fortune, to fund a series of institutions that would establish the top-down approach to social change that Powell recommended. The first of these, in 1973, was the Heritage Foundation, Weyrich's flagship organisation and arguably the most impor-tant. In 2017, the University of Pennsylvania ranked the Heritage Founda-tion the eighth most influential think tank in the world, and the only one in the top ten with an overtly ideological bent. Conservative media stars like Rush Limbaugh proudly cite the Heritage Foundation as the source of much of their research and ideas.

Hot on the heels of Heritage, Weyrich co-founded the American Legislative Exchange Council. ALEC, as it's more commonly known, is a non-profit group that allows conservatives in Congress to draft state-level model legislation in collaboration with the private sector, often based on ideas developed by the Heritage Foundation's thinkers. In 1974, Weyrich took another step with the Committee for the Survival of a Free Congress, ded-icated to training conservative grassroots activists, recruiting conservative political candidates and sourcing funding for conservative causes. Later, Weyrich became a founding member of the Council for National Policy (CNP), a networking forum for the wealthiest and most powerful conserv-atives in the US that was founded by the apocalyptic fiction writer Tim LaHaye. The CNP became an essential coordinating body for conservatives

as the lobbying industry grew in and around Washington DC during the
1980s and 1990s. Today, the CNP organises regular meetings for its members to discuss the day's most urgent conservative causes and broadly agree
how to tackle them.

The bottom-up and top-down pioneers have spawned a series of hugely
powerful networks at the county, state and national levels. They remain as
powerful and relevant today as when they were founded. Working together,
in 2010 they achieved their most decisive victory to date with one of the
Supreme Court of the United States' most controversial and divisive decisions in *Citizens United vs. the FEC*. In its aftermath, strategist Karl Rove
gleefully remarked: 'People call us a vast right-wing conspiracy, but we're
really a half-assed right-wing conspiracy. Now it's time to get serious.'

A large cast of characters directly and indirectly influenced this decision. Two in particular – Richard Viguerie of the bottom-up approach,
and Charles Koch of the top-down approach – proved to be the most
hard-working and biggest-spending activists in helping to achieve this
stunning conservative victory.

THE EVOLUTION OF GRASSROOTS POLITICAL NETWORKS

Two years after the triumphant meeting in Sharon, the Young Americans for Freedom had not yet quite happened. Though claiming a
membership of 25,000, they had only 2,000 paying members and were
$20,000 in debt. To raise money, Marvin Liebman hired a newly qualified
lawyer from Houston, Texas, gave him a list of 1,200 known conservative
donors and told him to start calling. After his first three calls, Richard
Viguerie had raised $4,500 and Liebman knew he'd found the right man for
the job.

To fundraise on a bigger scale, Viguerie took influence from the mail order
catalogue company Sears and Roebuck, *Readers Digest* magazine and Leo

8.2 *Richard Viguerie*

Burnett, the advertising agency that created the Marlboro brand. Each of
these companies had prospered by using 'direct mail' – marketing in the
form of a letter, addressed by name to the recipient, asking them if they'd
like to buy a product or magazine subscription, or pay to enter a lottery.
Viguerie's idea was to use direct mail to fundraise for conservative causes.

Viguerie and YAF used direct mail to raise money for Barry Goldwater's
1964 presidential campaign. The results were staggering. Though Goldwater lost the election he received close to one million individual contributions from working Americans (during the 1960 campaign Nixon had
received contributions from 50,000 individuals while JFK received funds

from just 22,000). The Goldwater contributions were for small amounts of money, but because so many people gave, the funding raised was substantial. Just as impressive was the number of volunteers involved. Heeding the Mao Tse Tung adage 'give me just two or three men in a village and I will take the village', the Goldwater campaign used direct mail to network effect, asking existing volunteers to contact people *they* personally knew with a plea to help out. Ultimately, four million people took part, and these volunteers contacted many millions more people. In contrast, Goldwater's opponent Lyndon Johnson had only half as many workers even though the Democratic voter pool was 50% larger.

Viguerie now understood that direct mail was not only good for fundraising, but could be used to construct an underground network that would amount to an organised grassroots conservative movement. Goldwater had inspired plenty of young conservatives to learn more about the conservative philosophy, and many of them were now studying techniques of political organisation. But nobody was studying how to *sell* conservatism to the American people. In 1965, Viguerie set up his own company to do just that.

Crucial to achieving this were his lists of conservative donors and volunteers – their names, addresses and occupations. Viguerie could measurably see that the efforts of people like Lemuel Boulware and Ronald Reagan on *GE Theater* were bearing fruit: his lists of committed conservatives included both blue-collar workers *and* their manufacturing bosses. Viguerie would spend the next fifty years building his lists. By his own estimation, Viguerie and Associates have sent in excess of two billion letters to conservatives across America, testing to see which messages, language and imagery have the greatest pull without having to use the mainstream media. Viguerie is now well into his eighties and still doing direct mail at the highest level for conservative candidates and causes: 'Today I have in my desk a book-size file of several hundred conservative mailing lists – they're the lifeblood of direct marketing.'

As technology has evolved in leaps and bounds, so too has direct marketing. Karl Rove, the political strategist who gave Lee Atwater his first job in Washington DC and would later mastermind George W. Bush's two successful presidential campaigns, was an early believer in the possibilities of technology-enhanced direct mail. He'd been a leader in the College Republicans during Nixon's 1972 campaign, and seen how essential opposition research and grassroots communications campaigns had been in giving Nixon his landslide victory. Rove's mantra, pinched from an IBM ad, was 'machines should work so people can think'. During the 2004 presidential elections, Rove and his team pioneered a new microtargeting tool. This involved building more comprehensive lists of demographic data, and developing algorithms that could make inferences about which people to target to encourage them to vote for their candidate:

> This complex analytical effort drew upon as many as 225 pieces of information we could collect on an individual household to help identify which members were likely to support Bush and turn out to vote for him. Among the pieces of information we sought were whether they owned a gun, whether their children attended private schools, what kind of magazines they subscribed to, what kind of car they owned, even what kind of liquor they preferred. No one piece of information was a reliable indicator by itself. The complicated algorithms that made sense of the relationships among these data points were prized secrets.

In 2010, Republican senate nominee Scott Brown took early advantage of the smartphone to make microtargeting effective in real time. Politicians have long understood that addressing local issues is the best way to motivate people to vote. Yet it was consumer data companies that worked out first how to use this accepted wisdom as a means to conversion. 'Location always is thought of as geographic,' explained retail analyst Michael Boland, but it's most valuable 'as a means toward building user profiles'. In other words, different issues might matter to two people who own guns, drive the same car, drink the same liquor and earn the same amount of money if they live in different parts of the country. Scott Brown's team used location-specific online ads to target voters across Massachusetts. His team also created a customer relationship management (CRM) app that allowed door-to-door vote canvassers to pull up a household's profile and see which ads they had been targeted with, so that the volunteer knew what to talk to them about. En route to the next house they could update the profile in the app with a summary of their conversation, letting other volunteers know whether they needed to re-canvas the house. With the help of this technology, Brown won an upset victory in a state that was once an established Democrat stronghold.

The advent of the social and mobile internet allowed microtargeting to highly specific networks to come into its own. Newt Gingrich, ever the future-focused ideas man, predicted in 1999: 'The internet will have an even bigger long-term impact than talk radio or TV commercials because of the underlying ability for people to sort of segment themselves into their niches through chat rooms and other interactive devices.' Early direct mail experimentation proved that extremist and hard-line messages were most effective for fundraising. 'Direct mail', said Morris Dees, the liberal direct mail maestro, 'only works on those people that have a pretty strong left or right ideological bent.' As the leaders of the world's most popular social networks have come to admit, extremism thrives online. The difference between direct snail mail and social media content is that the latter is far easier to share. Once again, conservatives are leading the way. A 2019 study by sociologist Jen Schradie found that, in the United States, conservatives are significantly more active online in issues-based groups than liberals.

Not everyone who joins an online issues-based group is ideological, but they are increasingly likely to come across extreme partisan content, par-ticularly in private online groups. Steady exposure leads to desensitisation, which has the effect of pulling people away from moderate positions. This, of course, is part of the radical conservative grassroots strategy.

TOP-DOWN TAKEOVER

Rich Fink first met his chief benefactor in the early 1970s. In response to a long-shot pitch for money, Charles Koch had agreed to meet with him. Charles was CEO of Koch Industries, originally an oil refining company and now the second largest privately owned conglomerate in the United States. Fink was a graduate student from New Jersey who showed up at Koch Industries' Wichita, Kansas HQ in a revolting black polyester suit with white piping. He asked Koch for $150,000 to fund a university course about the free market theories of the Austrian economists Friedrich Hayek and Ludwig von Mises. Koch enthusiastically agreed. Stunned, Fink asked him why he'd trust a long-haired, bearded student in a disco suit. Charles deadpanned, 'I like polyester. It's petroleum based.' With that, one of the most important conservative relationships of the past fifty years was cemented.

Charles, the eldest of four sons, inherited his father's place at the head of Koch Industries as well as his libertarian fanaticism. 'Charles' aim was to tear the government out at the root,' claimed Brian Doherty, an editor at the Koch-funded magazine *Reason*. A year after Paul Weyrich established the Heritage Foundation, Charles and his brother, David, founded the Cato Institute think tank. With that first taste of political funding, the Kochs realised they needed a more substantial plan. Rich Fink, taking a cue from both Weyrich and Charles' own leadership philosophy, Market-based Management, outlined a top-down approach in a white paper titled 'The Structure of Social Change'. Charles Koch immediately recognised and admired its production-line analogy: 'To bring about social change requires a strategy that is vertically and horizontally integrated. It must span idea creation to policy development to education to grassroots organisations to lobbying to political action.'

With the Cato Institute up and running, they went back to tackling education. Fink's Austrian economics programme was moved to uncelebrated George Mason University so that they could retain near total control over it. Renaming it the Mercatus Center, they forged a blueprint that underpins how the Kochs fund all their political initiatives, including at the more than 150 universities where they presently fund courses. Professor John Bednar explains: 'They have an immense amount of influence over who those professors are and what they teach and publish, and what research they do, and what they say in the classroom.'

The Kochs openly shrug off this criticism. 'If we're going to give a lot of money we'll make darn sure they spend it in a way that goes along with our intent,' says David.

To reach working Americans they set up Citizens for a Sound Economy (CSE). 'Great ideas are useless if they remain trapped in the ivory tower,' Charles believed. From 1984 until it closed shop in 2004, CSE, with Rich Fink as its president, became one of the most powerful funding and conservative coordinating forces in Washington DC. Its anti-tax efforts, in partnership with companies like Philip Morris and Exxon-Mobil, helped sweep Newt Gingrich and allies to power in the 1994 Congressional elections. By the time CSE was dissolved into Americans for Prosperity in 2004, the Kochs and their allies were building new organisations in a top-down network that would advance the Tea Party brand. Tea Party successes in the 2010 midterm elections resulted in President Obama extending billions in tax cuts to the very rich and retreating on reinstating a higher estate tax. But the true impact of these long-term efforts to influence politics can be measured in the way that United States as a whole has become more conservative. Though Tea Party conservatives made a big fuss about Obama being a 'socialist', in reality many of his policy ideas were conservative in origin. Conservative writer Henry Olsen even went as far to argue that 'Obama's rhetoric was closer to Reagan's than the rhetoric of Romney and many other leading Republicans in 2012'. To win with the electorate meant playing to the right.

The libertarian takeover of the Republican Party marked another dramatic change in conservative politics, akin to the 'great white switches' effected by Richard Nixon and Ronald Reagan in the 1970s and 1980s. Central to how this happened is the way that America's capital city has changed. To wield power in Washington you have to be able to do three things:

1. deliver a message and move people with it
2. attract dedicated followers to your cause
3. raise money to fund the effort required to do the first two things.

Many ambitious idealists and well-networked egotists can do the first two. It's far more difficult to raise money. The lobbying industry, which grew rapidly in response to the Watergate scandal and the growth in size of the federal government, has made fundraising more organised and methodical. Before Watergate, political consultancy was a vaguely dirty novelty that many politicians engaged in somewhat reluctantly as they geared up for an election campaign. After Watergate, when amendments to the Freedom of Information Act made it harder to hide how politics was done, political consultancy became an essential form of public relations. This coincided with large increases in staff employed by members of Congress. In 1959 there were 2,700 Senate staff; by the seventies there were 7,000. Staff numbers in the House of Representatives grew equally quickly, from 3,000 in 1960 to 9,300 by 1980. With more people to persuade in order to get access to politicians, and with more media channels through which to influence them, lobbyists became an unavoidable link in the DC food chain. In 1971 there were a couple of thousand registered lobbyists. By the mid eighties, that number had ballooned to 80,000. From Middle America, Charles quietly wrote cheque after cheque for specialist lobbyists. The dam burst when the Supreme Court opened the floodgates for unlimited anonymous political spending with their decision in *Citizens United vs. the FEC*.

The *Citizens United* case came from a complaint by the lobbying firm of the same name, who argued that if Michael Moore could make *Fahrenheit 9/11*, a commercial film with an overtly political message, then they should be able to do the same. Other courts had struck down their argument with the justification that commercial film companies can make political films simply because they're in the *business* of making films and, like any private organisation, don't need to disclose where the money needed to make the film came from. In contrast, lobbying firms can't make political films with donations from anonymous backers because the intention would so obviously be to influence how people vote. Citizens United argued that this was an infringement of free speech. The Supreme Court agreed. Journalist Jeffrey Toobin lambasted what this meant: '*Citizens United* gave rich people more or less free rein to spend as much as they want in support of their favoured candidate.' In the 2010 midterms in which Tea Party candidates did so well, lobbying groups spent $300 million – more than in every mid-term election combined since 1990.

8.3 *Charles Koch*

What can we learn from Case story 8?

Managing a team requires patience, energy and focus, particularly when it's a team of misfits who are trying to push forward change to create something new. Still, the nature of a team – a group of people working towards a common goal – gives it an inherent togetherness that should work to your advantage as you, the leader, cultivate and shepherd it forwards. Tapping into your networks for support is a totally different ball game. Teams don't succeed in a vacuum, and so using your networks will be essential to achieving your change vision. As you undoubtedly know – networks are hugely powerful things. They can be a benefit, as Case story 8 has shown, and the positive lessons to take away are:

- Energy and enthusiasm, particularly from younger people, can create momentum based on the power of the network effect. This results in communities coalescing spontaneously around an idea or person, which in turn generates more interest and support from new networks outside the immediate sphere.
- Older people like helping younger people to succeed. Their maturity and wisdom means their advice is likely to be balanced and considered, and they often have status and financial muscle that can clear obstacles and make things move faster.
- Interconnected networks that share common goals but that complement one another in terms of their different locations or expertise are more powerful than the sum of their parts. However, coordinating these networks so that they're holistically effective takes planning and foresight, and strong powers and levers of persuasion.

But it's also hard to foresee the unintended consequences that might come from calling on your networks for help, and far harder to control these unintended consequences than in a team scenario. In these circumstances they can be a hindrance. Watch out for:

- People going rogue. This could come from an overenthusiastic but naïve supporter doing something that offends other people you need onside, or a two-faced cynic who pledges support but then maliciously goes behind your back to stir shit up. When people go rogue you'll find yourself wasting energy on unnecessary and potentially embarrassing battles.
- Owing too many big favours. In your bid to realise your change vision you'll be in sales mode, jockeying for commitment and favours. This takes great mental and physical stamina, and it's easy to forget that people rarely do things for others entirely selflessly. The more powerful a person is, the more they're likely to expect in return – not necessarily because they're massively demanding and greedy (although, possibly they are), but because they're working with higher stakes. It can be an enjoyable challenge to have to repay one or two big favours, but very stressful to owe more than that.
- Conflicting interests. Once again, it's easy to fall into the trap of cognitive bias where, when drawing on your networks for support, you only see common goals and wilfully ignore the things you don't agree on. In a worst-case scenario, you could wreck your own progress by working with others who, by virtue of what they know and how they've helped you, end up forcing you into a position of ineffective compromise.

As ever, start by looking at your change plan and asking yourself what kinds of support you need from outside the team to make it successful. Often, I find the things people need from their networks fall into the following categories:

1. access to resources, such as people with particular skills or authority, or useful technologies;

2. advice and guidance, to help you overcome obstacles or avoid mistakes along the way;
3. the power to influence others to buy into your vision and champion it to their own networks;
4. community mobilisation, to inspire people over whom you have no direct influence to lend additional support and build momentum.

Once you've identified what you need, try to quantify it, even if it's only approximately. As you decide who could best help you with these needs, think about who they are, weighing up the possible benefits and hindrances, using the clues I've listed above and any other benefits and hindrances that you can think of that are particular to your circumstances. Plan how to approach them based on this, thinking about:

- From their perspective, how big is your ask? Is it something they can do without much breaking their stride or will they have to go out on a limb for you? The more onerous it is for them, the more you'll need to openly recognise this.
- How will you measure the usefulness of their help? Change isn't easy, and they're unlikely to be miracle workers. You may need to check in with them frequently and ask them to continue trying if, in the first instance (or second, or third), their efforts to help you don't deliver as anticipated. Warn them of this up front, so they know what to expect.
- Acknowledge what you can do for them. This takes self-awareness, not just of your abilities and resources, but also the residual benefits (and hindrances) that you might bring to them. Decide whether you should offer something specific in return or simply an open promise of a favour in return.
- What's your Plan B if, despite your best efforts to avoid them, some of those hindrances do occur? Hope for the best but plan for the worst, as they say.

Trump

Commandment

Apply all the commandments I've given so far to find your X Factor, which will make the impact of your change efforts greater than their sum.

Donald Trump is a conundrum. Media talkers are running out of adjectives to describe the extent of his idiocy, and yet he's president. He didn't even really want the job. How could this happen?

9.1 *On the campaign trail*

Trump was born and raised in Jamaica Estates, an affluent neighbourhood in suburban Queens, the borough of New York City most like small-town America. Five miles west, down Grand Central Parkway, the members of the punk band the Ramones burst out of working-class Forest Hills, born just a few years after Trump. New Yorkers – one and all. The definitive Ramones anecdote, in the words of their original drummer, Tommy Ramone, was one that captured the absurdity of their success:

> We were riding in our van and we made a rest stop at this restaurant, and after seeing us walk in, the owner of the place went up to our tour manager and said, 'It's so nice of you to be taking care of those retarded kids'. He was serious.

The unlikely story of how a gang of fools changed popular culture is so timeworn that it's passé. But the story of the Ramones' rise to cult legends offers clues as to how Donald Trump became president. Fundamentally, it's the same sort of story.

The Ramones looked ridiculous and each member was an oddball in their own peculiar way. Singer Joey had a crippling obsessive-compulsive disorder, bassist Dee Dee was a paranoid schizophrenic drug addict, and guitarist Johnny was an angry, bigoted control freak. Tommy was quiet and introverted. They weren't particularly fond of one another. Drummer Clem Burke, briefly a Ramone himself, said, 'The band had no chemistry. They all hated each other. That creates an anti-chemistry. Maybe that was part of their charm.' Johnny, a military-loving conservative, had an affair with Joey's girlfriend and eventually married her. In response, Joey, an awkwardly romantic liberal, wrote one of their best songs, 'The KKK Took My Baby Away', and nursed a lifelong grudge. They never spoke again, though they continued to play music together for the next fifteen years. 'To be in the Ramones you had to be miserable,' commented Dee Dee.

Yet the Ramones had something incredibly special. More so than Little Richard, Elvis Presley, the Beatles or Abba, the Ramones are the fount of modern pop music. People still craft artistic personas that resemble exaggerated cartoon characters; people still write songs that incorporate the same bone-headed R&B groove, dumbed-down melodies and irreverent lyrics. Ever since the Ramones created the look, the leather jacket, skinny jeans and Converse trainers combo has become, like a well-cut suit or a little black dress, that rarest of things: a timeless fashion. Their logo – a riff on the seal of the President of the United States – remains a reliable revenue stream for the large retail chains that license it to shift t-shirts and other accessories. The Ramones created a genre of music, a look and a brand. They may not have been stable geniuses, but they weren't stupid. From the beginning they knew they were on to something.

In the arts, when someone stands out head and shoulders above the competition we say they have an X Factor. It's referred to as an X Factor because it seems indefinable. But if you look long enough the X Factor can be distinguished. They connect with people and grab their attention, they entertain their audience and develop an emotional bond with them that *keeps* their attention, and they work hard to cultivate a business built around their creativity. Basically, they apply all of the commandments I've covered in the first eight case stories, and they do it so well that they seem to possess magic powers. Their X Factor proves that the impact they have is greater than the sum total of their efforts.

The Ramones knew their audience and crafted the Ramones personas based on this. Dee Dee acknowledged:

> We may have been a group based out of New York, but we were suburban people and we had the same problems everybody else has in Detroit or Ohio or anywhere else. They could relate to us. We were just the same as they were.

The Ramones' vision for their music was to take it 'back to the future'. Against the grain of the times, the Ramones wrote classic American pop songs in the vein of 1950s teenybopper music played with the straightforward aggression of 1960s garage rock. Their brand of entertainment was so simple yet so smart that it was prehistoric and futuristic at the same time.

Every channel of communication was considered to make sure that the impact they'd have on the audience would knock them sideways, from the lyrical content to the vocal sneer, from their performance posturing to the way their equipment was arranged to make the stage as compact as possible.

The Ramones and the people they employed were misfits, but they were immediately successful and were well networked with supporters in high places. They built a brilliant team around themselves, from artist Arturo Vega who designed the Ramones logo, to manager Danny Field who understood how to package them commercially, to tour manager Monte Melnick who kept them organised and alive as they toured incessantly, built a global fan base and changed popular culture for good.

Like the Ramones, Donald Trump has an X Factor. He has an X Factor because he instinctively and successfully follows all of the change commandments I've given so far. The Donald Trump presidency has been characterised as an 'American experiment', a collective wildcard vote to see if someone other than a political insider can solve the country's domestic and foreign problems. To borrow the words of author Michael Wolff, Trump is a Frankenstein creation of the conservative movement – 'the first, true, right-wing original'. It seems unlikely that this experiment will solve America's problems, but it's an experiment that's changed the culture of the American presidency for good.

So, the commandment for this case story is: Apply all the commandments I've given so far to find your X Factor, which will make the impact of your change efforts greater than their sum.

KING OF NEW YORK

In relation to change commandments one through three, Donald Trump intimately understands his voting base, the world of diminishing opportunities in which they live and the world they *want* to live in. His leadership persona is perfectly attuned to this.

9.2 *The Ramones*

The X Factor that Donald Trump and the Ramones share is a by-product of New York and the place that the city has in the American psyche. The original American experiment – a democracy as conceived by the founding fathers of the United States – was declared in Philadelphia, Pennsylvania, the country's original capital. But New York City, always the most populous in the union, is where the idea of modern America found its form.

The grubby French intellectual Jean Baudrillard concluded that 'only tribes, gangs, mafia families, secret societies and perverse communities can survive in New York'. This is a point of pride for New Yorkers, who revel in the idea that ambitious people have to get their hands dirty to succeed. It's why every Jay-Z album opens with a skit that casts the Brooklyn-born, Manhattan-conquering rapper as Scarface, Al Pacino's portrayal of a Cuban immigrant who turns himself into a millionaire drug lord; it's why mob funerals in New York are such solemnly glitzy media events; it's why the taint of scandal dogs so many New York area politicians, from former governor Eliot Spitzer (brought down by a prostitution scandal), to former congressman Anthony Wiener (brought down by an underage sex scandal), to former Goldman Sachs CEO and New Jersey governor Jon Corzine (indicted on several occasions for financial misdeeds). Donald Trump had this kind of persona dead in his sights when he ventured out of Queens to build grand hotels in Manhattan.

Trump, like the Ramones, hit Manhattan at its nadir in the mid 1970s. The city was bankrupt; its streets filthy, its authorities hopelessly corrupt. The journalist Legs McNeil evocatively captured the atmosphere of the time:

> It was the end of white flight in New York. People had been moving out of the city to the suburbs, so New York was kind of deserted and you really got this feeling that the parents had left and you could take over and do whatever you want.

Trump, eager to make his mark, knew from past experience that he'd have to contend with the city's well-oiled political machine. A political machine is a form of local government where a well-connected figure – a 'boss' – orchestrates who gets elected to office. They're able to persuade local communities to vote for their candidate because those communities rely on them for, say, jobs. In choosing to run as a Republican in 2016, Trump had to explain why 80% of his past political donations had been to Democrats in places like New York, Chicago and Atlantic City:

> I've got to do that. All these fucking Democrats run those cities. You've got to build hotels and grease them to do so. It's a rigged system. These guys have been shaking me down for years. There was a pol [politician] in Queens, an old guy with a baseball bat. You've got to give him something or nothing gets built. But if you take cash in there and you leave him an envelope, it happens. That's just the way it is.

Brought up to believe that business was unavoidably shady, Trump's organisation began to look increasingly like an organised-crime empire as his interests diversified. Russian, Panamanian and Azerbaijanian businessmen with dubious business interests of their own became his most important partners and clients. He carried that sense of the shadiness of power with him into politics. James Comey, the FBI Director that Trump fired soon after taking office, colourfully described his first impressions of Team Trump in 2016: 'I thought of New York Mafia social clubs, an image from my days as a Manhattan federal prosecutor in the 1980s and 1990s. The Ravenite. The Palma Boys. Café Giardino'. Later, at a private dinner at the White House, Comey recalled:

> Trump said, 'I need loyalty. I expect loyalty'. To my mind, the demand was like Sammy the Bull's Cosa Nostra induction ceremony – with Trump, in the role of the family boss, asking me if I have what it takes to be a 'made man'.

He wasn't Italian, but Trump was a dyed-in-the-wool New York gangster.

In 2016, Trump's political strategists Kellyanne Conway and Steve Bannon correctly predicted that this strongman-showman persona would strike a chord with blue-collar Americans for whom 'family' and 'honour codes' were everything. People whose family had, for generations, served in the military or been part of a labour union. People who loved violent outsiders, whose fictional heroes were characters like Tony Soprano, who had supported corrupt Democrat political machines because they brought working-class jobs to their communities. People whose Rustbelt cities or Bible Belt backwoods had now long been in decline.

Once, flying over Atlantic City in his private plane with an entourage, he offered to give a foreign model a tour of his casinos. The model's date, a billionaire friend of Trump's, balked at the idea of stopping off in a place overrun by white trash. 'What is this "white trash"?' the model asked. 'They're people just like me, only they're poor,' said Trump. It was a rare moment of deprecating self-awareness from which Trump's populist entertainer-politician persona was born. It's the kind of line that could've been said by Christopher Walken's anti-hero in the film *King of New York*. Frank White, a gangster fresh out of prison, decides he can clean up the crack-ridden streets and give back to his community by killing every single lesser crime lord, re-establishing his own criminal empire and then running for mayor.

THE ENTERTAINER

In relation to commandments four through six, Trump has created a powerful 'back to the future' vision that resonates emotionally with his audience and offers a promise they believe in. He creatively uses a variety of communications channels and rhetorical styles to keep his audience entertained and engaged.

Trump's 'back to the future' change vision is based on an intoxicating belief that a beneficent universe smiles down on a chosen people. By literally erecting bigger barriers to entry – a crackdown on illegal immigration and the construction of a border wall with Mexico, higher import trade tariffs, the repatriation of tax dollars earned by American multinationals overseas and the jobs they currently export to cheaper labour markets – Trump aims to change the national economy and culture back to a time when being born an American meant a significant advantage in the world.

The components of his new Conservative Populism Narrative read something like this:

Protagonists: decent, patriotic Americans;
Antagonists: cynical elites, particularly the media, that profit from denigrating America
Genesis: social and economic breakdown in post-industrial America;
Change catalyst: an anti-politician, proudly un-PC candidate standing for president – and winning;

Adventure: taking bold, unorthodox actions that deliberately agitate liberals while demonstrating strength and power;

Outcome of adventure: recreating the America of the 1950s, when it was more racially stratified and more sedate, and GDP was more equally distributed (without giving up the modern-conveniences developed over the intervening 70 years);

Promise: America regains its position as the undisputed world leader, a place where opportunity and wealth for all go hand in hand and confidence and optimism are restored to the national culture;

Newfound purpose: To Make America Great Again.

Much of this vision is credited to Steve Bannon, who saw Trump as the perfect vessel for his ideas. For as much appeal as it has to certain types of American women (and it does), it's a fundamentally male vision in which a self-confident, non-conformist American hero does battle with everything that stands in his way: a man with the common touch but otherworldly powers. If Bannon was, ideally, looking for the Marlboro Man, Trump was a good second best. He had that New York showmanship, a strange hybrid of booming authority that took over the room and a regular guy in a bar yelling at the TV. Importantly, Trump shared this vision and could authentically make it part of his repertoire.

Trump's abilities as an entertainer are also an important source of his X Factor, and certainly a reason he rode the populist wave of 2016 to victory while Bernie Sanders faltered. Trump's entertainer credentials were honed out of necessity. Between the mid 1980s and mid 1990s, his company lost over a billion dollars. If he once was a billionaire, he was now, humiliatingly, forced to simply act out the role in TV ads for fast food, in a cameo at Wrestlemania billed as 'The Battle of the Billionaires' (in which he 'clotheslines' wrestling mogul Vince McMahon and forcibly shaves his head), and in his steady gig as reality TV host of *The Apprentice*. From these inauspicious beginnings, Trump's remarkable second act was forged. Not only was his newfound celebrity lucrative, but it also helped him connect with the people who would vote him into power.

Monumental self-belief defined Trump's first act. That was a product of his regular attendance in his youth at the Marble Collegiate Church in Manhattan, then under the ministry of Reverend Norman Vincent Peale. While there, Peale published *The Power of Positive Thinking*, a hugely successful self-help book that influenced a variety of politicians, business leaders, sports stars and televangelists, as well as the development of self-improvement techniques like neuro-linguistic programming (NLP). Trump credits Peale for teaching him to 'accentuate the positive and eliminate the negative', which helped him bounce back from bankruptcy in the 1990s (he also claimed that Peale 'thought I was his greatest student of all time'). Michael Wolff pinpointed this self-belief as the primary element of Trump's X Factor: 'One of his extraordinary gifts is to be able, in the midst of huge failure, to declare victory.'

Post bankruptcy, Trump came to see success as a divine right. Steve Bannon saw in him this yearning to believe that being American should mean that a little effort can lead to big success:

> Trump was the guy who never went to class. The night before the final, he comes in at midnight from the fraternity house, puts on a pot of coffee, takes your notes, memorises as much as he can, and gets a C. And that's good enough. He's going to be a billionaire.

This idea that opportunity should come easy appeals to a sense of frustrated hardship that stretches beyond the country's borders. 'I didn't come to the United States to bust my fuckin' ass, man,' says Tony Montana in *Scarface*. To union men and women facing the ignominy of having to retrain for service jobs that pay lower wages than their old manufacturing jobs, this idea of divined success was a promise to believe in. To Americans weaned on Rush Limbaugh, the man responsible for the dumbing down of conservative entertainment, Trump's outrageous entitlement was a sign of greatness. He didn't read because he didn't have to – he was rich. Following the lineage of conservative media entertainers, Trump was an obvious heir apparent. He was a conservative entertainer for a social media age.

A fascinating finding from Jonathan Haidt's research into the foundations of morality was that self-identified liberals prioritise just three of these foundations:

1. Care/Harm
2. Fairness/Cheating
3. Liberty/Oppression.

That is, they vote for politicians and support policies that emphasise equality of opportunity and a caring approach to the more vulnerable sectors of society. Self-identified conservatives, however, prize all six of the moral foundations equally:

1. Care/Harm
2. Fairness/Cheating
3. Loyalty/Betrayal
4. Authority/Subversion
5. Liberty/Oppression (conservatives tend to emphasise freedom of choice for this foundation, rather than equality of opportunity)
6. Sanctity/Degradation.

Haidt's interpretation of this was that conservatives have a bigger emotional palette to reference, which is probably why they've been so successful in shifting America to the right. Trump has mastered how to draw on this palette. At his campaign rallies, often held in old, faded sports arenas that evoked past glories and underscored the wretchedness of the country's industrial decline, Trump spoke in the emotional, experiential and unscripted style of Christian evangelism, expertly taking the temperament of the crowd in the moment. Establishment critics, used to hearing polished, slippery platitudes from politicians, dismissed his rhetoric as unsophisticated. But Trump was doing all the right things:

- speaking to the magnets and wedge issues that emotionally resonated with his audience – the issues that separated them from liberals;

- using transgressions unearthed via opposition research to attack his opponents in the emotional manner of a boxer psyching himself up and his opponent out;
- drawing powerfully on conservative American symbolism and drama to make promises about making America great again;
- strategising in public about policy execution that communicated transparency of thought and commitment to change that could whip his audiences into a frenzy.

Kellyanne Conway told Trump she believed he'd win even when everyone else believed it was impossible: 'You get these massive crowds where you have not erected a traditional political campaign. You have built a movement. And people feel like a part of it.'

Trump built on this by dominating non-traditional comms channels in his inimitable style. He spontaneously dialled into radio shows, appeared in comedy skits on Jimmy Fallon's *Tonight* show (sample Q&A: 'How are you going to create jobs in this country?' – 'I'm just going to do it') and answered questions in real time on Reddit. Most strikingly, he's developed a unique voice on Twitter around which his presidency has essentially been built. 'This is my megaphone, the way that I speak directly to the people without any filter. It's the reason I got elected,' he told aides who were horrified at his inability to communicate diplomatically and 'presidentially'. Once again, Trump knows what he's doing. Early in his presidency he analysed his past tweets, looking for common themes, popular subject matter and effective language. He realised that his most effective tweets were the most shocking or outrageous ones. He realised that a contempt for facts meant that it was difficult to pin charges of lying or dishonesty on him. 'I've made up stuff forever and they always print it,' he bragged of his brazen willingness to manipulate the press. As time's progressed, people have stopped batting much of an eyelid. After all, it's just entertainment.

9.3 *Steve Bannon and Kellyanne Conway*

CHAOS MAGICK LEADERSHIP

In relation to commandments seven and eight, Trump has built a messily effective team of misfits around him that supports his anti-presidential leadership style. A born manipulator, he plays different networks of entrenched interests off against one another to navigate his way from one crisis to the next.

As the Trumps settled into the White House and the Donald's administration took shape, his staff quickly came to believe two things about their boss:

1. he didn't live in the real world
2. he might have powers beyond their comprehension.

He believed he had more power and authority than he did, as president, have, and he was way too overconfident about his abilities to control and manipulate people. By any well-regarded measure of leadership he was terrible – undisciplined, incapable of strategic thought or action, totally self-focused with no loyalty to the people who worked for him, though he demanded total fealty from them. Yet here he was – a bullshit artist who for much of his life had run either a criminal or at least semi-criminal enterprise (the jury was out, though no one believed it was completely above board) – as POTUS (President of the United States). He must know something about power and success that they didn't. It was another sign of his indefinable X Factor.

Trump is a lifelong insider-outsider. His resentment of liberal elites began when upper-crust Manhattanites mocked him, in society magazines, for being so conspicuously successful, and then mocked him even more when his businesses began to fail. Their snobbery and hypocrisy contributed greatly to the chip that Trump carries on his shoulders, but it also helped him refine his strangely effective style of 'chaos magick' leadership. Chaos magick is a form of mysticism that has a lot in common with self-help and the idea that a person can will things to happen through the power of self-belief. Through a self-help lens, it's quite a modest idea: positive thinking is self-motivational and attractive to others, which influences them to help you succeed. Through a chaos magick lens, the idea becomes much more grandiose: a strong practitioner could have the mental power to influence a collective doubting of objective reality.

Trump has been trying to create reality ever since he set his sights on being a Manhattan real estate mogul, offering gossip to tabloid reporters about New York society parties so long as they always referred to him as 'billionaire Donald Trump' in their columns. In his books he elaborates on his approach to business, a blend of the soft power he learned from Norman Vincent Peale (self-belief) and the hard power he learned from the political machines of America's biggest cities (being gangster):

Self-belief	Being gangster
'I play it very loose. I prefer to come to work each day and just see what happens.'	'My style of deal-making is quite simple and straightforward. I aim very high, and then I just keep pushing and pushing and pushing to get what I'm after.'
'I like thinking big. Most people think small, because most people are afraid of success, afraid of making decisions, afraid of winning.'	'One of the keys to thinking big is total focus – a controlled neurosis. It's great when it comes to getting what you want. This is particularly true in New York real estate, where you are dealing with some of the sharpest, toughest, and most vicious people in the world.'
'I don't hire a lot of number-crunchers, and I don't trust fancy marketing surveys. I'm a great believer in asking everyone for an opinion. I ask and I ask and I ask, until I begin to get a gut feeling about something. And that's when I make a decision.'	'Be strategically dramatic. New York City hit us with an enormous tax assessment. We sued the city for $500 million. The lawsuit saved us $97 million. We never would have gotten any of it if we hadn't taken dramatic action.'

Trump's modus operandi is to do things that undermine elite notions of accepted practice, in essence saying: 'the truths that reinforce your cultural beliefs are wrong, because I exist. I'm the exception that disproves your rules.' If good government is about discipline and method, Trump's government has been set up to be chaotic and mad. Decisions are made on the fly, ideas are thrown at the wall to see which will stick, policy positions flip-flop constantly. Cultural change is messy and unpredictable, which, like a pig in shit, is how Trump likes it.

His administration is staffed with a rotating cast of misfits who represent the networks of interest that helped him win power, from establishment Republicans (chiefs of staff Reince Priebus and John Kelly), to populist conservatives (political consultants Steve Bannon and Kellyanne Conway), and even liberal elites (daughter Ivanka and her husband, Jared Kushner). Like a political machine boss of old, Trump rejects the organisation charts of the White House that show formal reporting lines. As far as he's concerned, everyone works directly for him. This causes vicious infighting between the different factions as they jockey for influence over the president. To

Priebus, who saw people like Bannon, Conway, Ivanka and Jared as 'natural predators', this was why nothing much got done. Trump's standard retort to generally accepted ways of doing politics or crafting policy is a blunt: 'that's too establishment'. He likes the aggressive disagreements, because they smoke out a variety of opinions and disrupted groupthink. Much as he disliked Trump's way of doing things, Priebus had to admit, 'Trump uses leverage over other people in a way I've never seen before.'

From the outset, Trump was also keen to demonstrate to the world that networks of political and bureaucratic power would be subservient to him. After he won the election, Washington insiders were forced to endure the classic New York 'perp walk', making the pilgrimage to Trump Tower in front of the press if they wanted an audience with the president-elect (a perp walk is when the police parade a suspected perpetrator of a crime before the media following their arrest). At a televised celebration of America's law enforcement agencies, Trump invited leaders from various agencies to hug him in full view of the cameras. James Comey's horrified view was that Trump seemed to be asking these civil servants, for whom political allegiance is considered both unprofessional and unpatriotic, to 'kiss his ring', showing deference and loyalty. He's used threats of executive privilege to subvert the authority of Congress, and exploited the partisan divide between the two political parties to cajole Republicans to fall in line behind him, even when they don't agree with his views or behaviour. A second term in office, unthinkable not too long ago, now looks very possible.

What can we learn from Case story 9?

To find your X Factor and make the impact of your change efforts greater than their sum, you need to do some Overton Window thinking.

As populism has swept the globe over the past several years, the Overton Window has become one of the most referenced concepts of socio-political change. Joe Overton, an executive at the Mackinac Center, a conservative think tank in Michigan, developed it in the 1990s. Overton suggested that public policies could be arranged on a spectrum of more or less government intervention, with the two opposing extremes being anarchy and totalitarianism (in proposing a spectrum of more or less government intervention he was deliberately trying to avoid comparison with the left–right political spectrum). At a given moment in time, a window of possibility exists along this spectrum. Policies within the window are socially acceptable enough to be debated and considered. There'll still be disagreement about which of these policies should become law, but hey – that's democracy. Policies outside the window are unthinkable.

Overton believed that the public decides what's acceptable. Hence the important role of institutions like think tanks and the media to influence the public to move the window towards more or less government intervention around a particular policy issue. He argued that the way to influence the movement of the window was to propose extreme ideas that lie at the end of the spectrum to which you want the window to move. A libertarian like Overton therefore might propose that the government should have no role in funding education. This was an extreme idea that he knew would

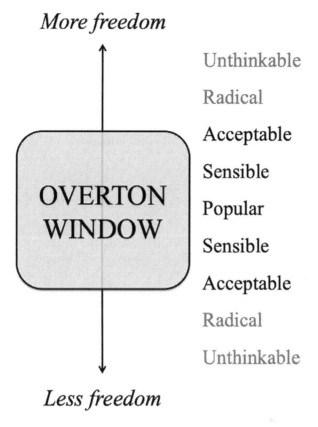

More freedom

Unthinkable

Radical

Acceptable

Sensible

OVERTON
WINDOW

Popular

Sensible

Acceptable

Radical

Unthinkable

Less freedom

9.4 _The Overton Window_

never fly, but it could influence the public to move the window to consider previously unacceptable ideas like reducing regulation around home schooling. Overton was describing the results of the assembly line theory of social change as developed by fellow conservatives like Paul Weyrich and Rich Fink. Their efforts had successfully helped America become a more conservative society during the latter half of the 20th century.

In the 21st century, as America has become a significantly more divided country, the Overton Window has essentially been stretched. The window isn't moving towards more or less government intervention so much as it's widening to include more extreme ideas at both ends of the spectrum. Donald Trump has actively helped stretch it at both ends – towards more government intervention in terms of trade tariffs and immigration control, and towards less government intervention in terms of lowering taxes and reducing regulation, as well as tacitly recognising the legitimacy of hate speech and the like. He's a master of proposing outrageously extreme ideas, like, to pick just one, buying Greenland from Denmark. This is fundamentally why his presidency has been so effective at effecting culture change.

The Overton Window concept is also used in business as an innovation tactic. Like anyone, inventors and entrepreneurs can't help but be constrained by what's considered reasonable (and by 'reasonable' I mean scientifically possible, ethical and/or socially acceptable). To come up with novel ideas it's important to mentally shift your window of perspective on what's reasonable in the area in which you're working. A good example of this is vegetarian food. For a long time, vegetarian food was considered either foods that weren't meat (i.e. vegetables, fruit etc.) or meat-like products that were manufactured from meat substitutes (e.g. burgers made from wheat protein). But Overton Window thinking is trying to shift that, by proposing extreme ideas like growing meat in a lab. If the meat was never alive, who's to say it's not vegetarian-friendly? In this way, over time, lab-produced meat products could expand the vegetarian population to make a meaningful impact on reducing climate change.

If you've applied all of the commandments so far you'll have a plan for implementing your change vision. But because it's been so sensitive to what your people want and will accept, it likely sits safely inside your organisation's Overton Window. That's good in some ways – it's realistic and achievable. But it's bad in others – for all your efforts to make it exciting and entertaining, it's still probably a little dull. To spice the plan and your own profile up a little, you need to come up with one or two extreme ideas that truly capture the imagination and incite some controversy.

Obviously, these ideas should be extreme destinations in the direction of change you're going. In Case story 5 I used the example of a change vision focused on setting your people free so that they can experiment with new ideas that will allow them to better fulfil their creative urges (i.e. simplifying a process by getting rid of unnecessary sign-off procedures and flattening your team's organisational structure). An example of extremes outside the Overton Window for this could be:

- abolishing job descriptions and titles entirely, so everyone can decide individually how to create value for the organisation and develop performance measures against which their success is judged;
- redecorating the office to resemble a science fiction future where nothing is permanent and any kind of behaviour is acceptable.

Clearly these are ludicrous ideas and they shouldn't be championed apropos of nothing. But with the support of your change sponsor within the organisation, they *should* be discussed and debated. For example, you could commission the creation of a video that shows a future version of your organisation where job descriptions and titles don't exist, with vignettes highlighting how this has made people more creative but also thrown up some challenges. Or you could host a hackathon where teams are set the challenge of designing the sci-fi office redecoration. The point isn't to try and get people to come round to these ideas completely, but to encourage debate and subtly communicate that this kind of radical thinking is needed. The more open minded people are, the more likely they will accept and help implement your change vision.

Importantly, people will see you in a new light. Less a competent but slightly dull executive and more of a free-thinking visionary who also happens to be approachable, empathetic and capable of creating real value for the organisation. The kind of person who people say has an indefinable X Factor.

EPILOGUE

What is the number one mistake that change leaders make at the outset of a culture-change programme? In my view, it's that they focus on the wrong kinds of change outside the organisation to justify why change is needed *within* the organisation. They cite challenging economic conditions, or market uncertainty, or the changing nature of the competition. Senior leaders whose political masters are shareholders or partners or government ministers have been taught that this is what their audience wants to hear. It's always struck me as strange, because it's not like it's easy to influence the macro economy.

The people who determine whether a change programme is successful are not shareholders, partners or government ministers. They're employees and customers. The kind of outside change that a leader should use as a guide for their change programme is the zeitgeist. That's the kind of change that affects people at an individual level, that influences our worldviews and how we behave. *Zeitgeist* is a German word that means 'spirit of the age', which is a poetic way of saying 'the culture of society'. As a reference for designing a culture-change programme, the zeitgeist eats economic uncertainty for breakfast simply because you're closer to the source of what matters to people. Economic conditions, changing industries and technological progression *influence* culture, but the zeitgeist literally *is* culture.

It's not a new idea that business leaders should use the zeitgeist as a decision-making guide. That it's still not that popular, despite being championed by venture capitalists like Peter Thiel and Vinod Khosla, and thinkers such as Malcolm Gladwell and Nicholas G. Carr, is probably because it's difficult to measure. The overwhelming gospel of science and data that dominates organisational thinking in the West – a zeitgeist in itself – discourages using your instincts for strategic decision-making. You could, of course, measure the zeitgeist – there are stats for just about everything. The problem is that there's no guide for which data to use, which means you have to call on committees to help you decide, and by the time they've written their report the zeitgeist, like tobacco smoke in a noisy room, has dissipated into something else.

'Liberalism', said the Supreme Court Justice William O. Douglas, 'is the spirit that is not too sure it's right.' Coincident with the rise of conservatism in the United States over the past 50 or so years, the Western organisation has become increasingly liberal, in favour of open trade and individual diversity. Douglas' comment speaks to the strengths of liberalism – adaptive, positive in outlook while ever questioning what's right – but also its weaknesses. It simply lacks the courage of its convictions. Perhaps this is because liberalism is, at a global level, quite rare. In a 2010 academic paper, three behavioural scientists bemoaned the 'broad claims about human psychology and behaviour based on samples drawn entirely from Western, Educated, Industrialised, Rich and Democratic (WEIRD) societies'. WEIRD people make up something like 10% of the world's population, and that percentage is declining. Not all WEIRD people are liberal (many, as we've seen, are quite conservative), but the vast majority of liberals in the world are WEIRD. Being a liberal is a bit like being an endangered species, the remainder of whom congregate in glass and concrete fortresses in the nicest parts of big Western cities and practise a curious kind of cognitive dissonance: lamenting the zeitgeist (and adverse economic conditions) while refusing to acknowledge it because it can't be sensibly measured. Meanwhile, in the slums and fields and humdrum suburbs, masses of people, often quite demographically diverse themselves, turn to stranger and more extreme versions of conservatism.

Organisations are obsessed with change. Like restless insomniacs they toss and turn, trying to get comfortable, but the bed never feels right and blessed rest just won't come. They wear down their resources trying to make change work, weakening the organism as a whole. People get demoralised and leave. The culture doesn't change so much as the people do. The methods and frameworks and metrics we use to design and implement and measure change need to radically change. If they ever were, they're no longer fit for purpose.

Why? Because the zeitgeist. We live in a world where two completely opposing ideas can be reliably called the truth, because there's no shortage of experts with copious amounts of data who'll advocate for one idea or the other (the biggest-selling book of all time about data analysis is quite correctly titled *How to Lie with Statistics*). We live in pluralistic societies where people form relationships across communities that have completely different beliefs about what's right and wrong, what's acceptable and what's not. Every person has at least two public personas – their real world self, governed mostly by reason and decorum, and their online self, governed mostly by emotion and contradiction. The media used to be a thing we turned on occasionally throughout the day – now it's something we rarely turn off.

Over the past five years or so it's struck me that people who champion conservative ideas understand people and the way the world is changing better than self-identified liberals. They're better at influencing and persuading people. They're less interested in measuring economic conditions and more interested in tapping into the zeitgeist. On balance, globally, they're in the ascendant. 'Liberalism has become obsolete,' crowed Russia's Vladimir Putin in a June 2019 interview with the *Financial Times*. To which a chorus of uncertain liberal voices meekly called back something unintelligible.

As a typically self-doubting liberal I find myself increasingly drawn to conservatism, less because I agree with its positions and more because I like its rebellious overconfidence. Particularly in America, its 'turn back the clocks and stop time' connotations are a bit of a red herring: it's always been a pragmatic ideology that's fiercely obsessed with winning the future. Like a 'back to the future' narrative should, it simply references the past for propulsive power. With a few fringe exceptions, it's liberalism in America that's stuck in the past.

Conservatism's rebellious overconfidence may, in the end, kill it. In the meantime we can, like good little WEIRDos, analyse why it works, apply our findings, decide how to measure whether we're doing it right – or, fuck that, just instinctively follow its crazy lead, feeling our way into the future.

INDEX

Page entries in **bold** refer to tables.